New Wave Nordic Skiing!

XC Breakthroughs & the Liberation of Winter

by Jeff Potter

Out Your Backdoor Press

ISBN 10 1-892590-63-8

ISBN 13 978-1-892590-63-3

Copyright 2018

Library of Congress Control Number 2018959196

Books may be ordered by sending $25 each, postpaid, to:
Out Your Backdoor, 4686 Meridian Rd., Williamston MI 48895

Order a full-color eBook version in either EPUB or Kindle format
by sending $15 via PayPal to jeff@outyourbackdoor.com

Also available on Amazon (print and Kindle) and at select bookstores and ski shops.

Email jeff@outyourbackdoor.com
(PayPal is accepted at this email address.)

For more information on XC skiing, or on other OYB articles and books,
visit OutYourBackdoor.com, also visit the Outyourbackdoor channel at YouTube.

PHOTO CREDIT: Many photos in this book were taken by my brother Tim Potter. Thanks!

Contents

*Thank you Martha for your patience while I ski
...and while I wrote this book.*

And thanks Woody for your guru-quality advice.

Jump Right In!

"Yeee-haaa! Wooo-hooo!" That's what anyone can hear from my friends around here when we get our first good snowfall each year. It's because they're going skiing again. And they don't have to go far to experience all the ski joy they can handle.

Where our little ski gang lives is like a lot of places in snow country: after a few weeks of freezes in fits and starts the ground gets hard and soon some snow falls. We might not get a lot, but a few inches is enough for us to experience a lot of heaven while still on earth.

After all, skiing is simply sliding around and playing on snow. It's glide, rhythm and flow. ...And that's all it takes to make a human smile!

Who? What? Why?

This book isn't a How-to, it's a Why-to. It's for YOU! So few people ski and play in their everyday local snow that if these ideas and innovations inspire you, you'll be a special part of today's new wave in XC — an early adopter!

It sure feels like a fresh, new wave to us, because the first time it snows every winter we can't believe our luck — especially in light of cool new gear and the sweet places we can now ski thanks to it, and due to our new attitudes and fresh skills! We think that the more people who know about it all, the bigger the wave will rise!

It's time for a new look at XC skiing, with a viewpoint that knows how to adapt to climate change realities. And it's time to promote the big changes in skiing technology that have been overlooked. And it's time to encourage a new attitude to snow among a lot of people who live around it. And a fresh attitude to skiing even among experienced skiers. And it's time to teach a wider range of techniques, especially so everyone can enjoy the simple trails that are closest to most of us.

This book is for never-ever's who don't yet "get" snow or XC. And it's also for experienced skiers who've probably not yet explored trail skiing.

I don't like to dwell on "winter." Snow country usually gets a month of snow AFTER winter. Spring is warm and sunny and it's also a ski season! But this isn't promoted nearly enough.

In this book I'll explain how it is for me and my friends in Michigan. We've skied a lot of other places, too. We've transformed our winter worlds using these ideas. Let's see what they can do for you.

It's also time for XC to reach out to today's most gung-ho winter trail users : the snowbikers. And to explain what trail skiing is to people who might be really receptive: mt-bikers. These people famously love their singletrack. The newsflash is that trail skiing is a thing and there's now a "mt-bike of skis."

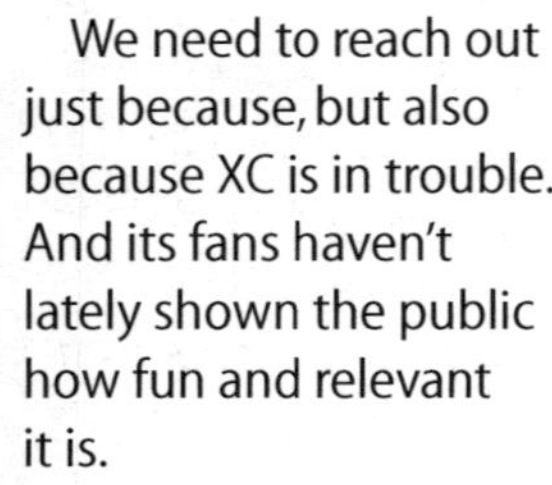

We need to reach out just because, but also because XC is in trouble. And its fans haven't lately shown the public how fun and relevant it is.

XC had a first wave: it used to be REALLY popular. Even though the gear was REALLY primitive! ...It's high time for a New Wave!

I was one of the first zinesters back in the 90's. We published zines because the mainstream wasn't expressing the reality we knew. This book has that same amateur DIY punk-rock attitude.

Other ski books are set in famous ski locations and are officially endorsed and published as part of some mainstream sports series. They promote the status quo. ...Which has got XC into its current situation, which is people not knowing how fun it is.

Hey, where are the mountains, some of you might ask? If you flip through this book, you might notice a lack of "out west" settings that dominate most ski media. Don't worry! Snow is snow, the world around. This is a homemade book and I live in the Midwest. You'll have to translate what we're doing with our snow to your own. It shouldn't be too hard. Most snow people don't live out west, anyway. Western snow country is high elevation and sparsely populated. It's not such a big deal for a neighborhood sport like XC skiing. The west is cool, but it's for special trips. This is a meat'n'taters book. XC skiing is ideally suited to helping the most people have the most fun since we can do it anywhere there's snow. My focus is on places that have the most snow for the most people. Sadly, those places are now getting less snow, but I'll show you how we don't let that slow us.

Everyone knows books are passe' today. Also, less is more. So it's nervy of me to produce an extensive book for such a simple sport. It's true that all I'm aiming at is the simple mission of getting folks outside having fun in the snow. A few chapters should be enough, right?

Well, winter and skiing are actually complicated, and unpublicized breakthroughs abound in most of the many technology aspects of this sport. I want to show how each detail can be used for liberation. That takes more pages rather than fewer.

I hope this book can inspire you. It's meant to give a taste of many of the aspects that make up the coolness of everyday low-overhead XC. It's not really a how-to -- except I do explain a few trail skiing moves you won't find anywhere else. If you how-to details, dang-nabbit, just google it.

Like, you don't have to give a rip about waxing, but it can turn casual skiing into a magic carpet ride, so I'm sharing just a few of the nifty parts of its lore. But don't let that distract you: you can fuggitaboutit and just go skiing. Or you can go way deeper down that rabbit hole online.

I'm pretty sure that any Nordic revival has to happen courtesy of regular folks. I'm giving you enough material to work with. Because since the big 1970's boom in XC skiing, most shops have closed, and XC is barely promoted. We're on our own.

Who are We?

We're just people who live where it snows. When snow happens, since we like to have fun, we do the obvious thing that literally millions of people around the world do who live in snow country: we go skiing!

Skiing isn't hard or easy. It's just something for people. You qualify!

But to really learn you need an instructor, though YouTube videos are awesome. My videos on the Outyourbackdoor channel are designed especially for regular folks -- they are totally DIY yet they have the most views of how-to XC vids!

My goal is to show a fresh way to think about skiing -- to show how it can be yours, now. In my view, looking behind the curtain, remembering where we've come from, and checking out related scenes and how they've handled change are all part of understanding what we're up to.

Yeah, this is only my view, and it might be limited to one part of the USA in some ways, but snow is snow and fun is fun, so hopefully it'll give you some inspiration no matter where you live.

Here We Go!

Like a zine, this book was unpublishable. The only market in ski books is for how-to, and that only microscopically. The one that is in print is all the usual market can bear. So I'm doing it myself.

You might notice that some of the photos here are a bit unprofessional (lots of rear-views), especially the selection: a lot of them are of me! (And my friends.) Well, I can't afford to buy photos or hire work. They're all I have. Many of the ones of me are taken by my brother Tim who is a lifelong photographer. People who can ski AND shoot achieve an amazing split-focus trick that I usually can't.

I also understand that books are passe'. But I'll publish in paper anyway, quixotic as that may be, and also as an eBook with full-color photos. I'll also publish updates at my OYB website and post new videos to my OutYourBackdoor YouTube channel.

I hope that readers use my Amazon Affiliate info when they shop there. I'll be giving examples of great gear that I use, and links to Amazon. They'll send me 4-8% of anything you purchase on that whole visit, any time you use the OYB affiliate URL suffix: /jeffpottersou-20. Just add that to the end of whatever you're looking at and click return and when you order they'll send me some $ at no cost to you.

Ironically, while public awareness of XC is at its lowest, more info about it is available than ever. Hopefully, this book inspires you to dig around if you have more questions! Also, go find the ski shop nearest to you and work with them to get the rig you need! Then take some lessons!

XC skiing is one of the things I know, so I'll do what I can to help.

What is Skiing?

Our sport is so surrounded by confusion, stereotype, bias and reduced straits that it helps to go back to basics to understand it. --What is a definition of skiing where if you removed anything you wouldn't be skiing? This one makes the most sense to me:

Skiing is action on snow with glide, rhythm, and pay-off.

I'll explore this concept in detail in the Experience chapter.

But What *Kind* of XC Skiing?

XC has an identity problem, always has. It has other names -- Cross-country, Nordic... But most of us when asked where we're going will answer "out skiing!"

Really, all skiing is one big family.

As for names, it gets worse: when you get into skate-skiing it doesn't even have names, it has numbers!

Name confusion is bad for marketing and even affects popularity. Names matter!

Downhill only has "alpine" as another name. Snowboarding has riding to mess up and lengthen any description of snowsport. Mountain-biking is only sometimes in the mountains but it's cool and spelling it "mt-biking" or "mt-biking" doesn't seem to hurt.

All these other sports, and probably even trail-running, have a reputation for being cool and fast. XC's general public vibe is slow and boring. Why? Can we fix this?

Where is XC From?

XC came from the Scandinavian countries as "just plain skiing." It's over 1000 years old and was used to make snow travel easier. Snowshoes are older yet. In the US, immigrants brought skiing to the Sierras for the 1800's Gold Rush and then wherever else Nordic people emigrated to, like Minnesota and the rest of the Midwest.

All skiing at first had a free heel so skiers could get up hills. In alpine regions linked turns and gear were developed to have fun while staying in control down long mountain slopes. Scandinavians worked more on techniques for long distance skiing.

From the first, skiing was used both for utility and play. Early competitions were typically "skimeister" blends of distance, jumping, and downhilling.

In the 1940's ski lifts let alpine skiers fix their heels for more control. Once heels were locked down, alpine skiers became shackled to the lifts and small scopes of horizontal travel. They fixated on linked turns.

Laminating let Nordic skiers make lighter skis with an arched mid-section to keep the kickwax off of the snow for more speed. Kickwaxes were developed to give grip and glide in a wide range of snow types. Before the arched "double camber"

ski, Nordic skis were used for both traveling and turning. Once distance speed was unleashed, linked turning became awkward and was given over to fixed heel skis ... until the 1970's when freeheel telemark skiing was rediscovered and XC skiing made comebacks for both speed and turns.

My Pitch

You might think that skiing is straightforward, like any hobby, like inline skating or windsurfing, say. That it's a consumer activity. It can be a trend, a fad. Maybe it's popular for awhile but then might fade. ...That it's a lot like deciding to go to the gym or not. But there's more to it. We don't have to be content with the one wave we've had! It's time for another!

When you engage XC skiing you encounter a mixed bag and a bit of social schizophrenia. You might wonder "Why can't I buy gear where I live?" Or "Why do skiers leave town to ski? There's snow right here." I'll fill you in on this. At least from my typical winter town vantage. You're not the crazy one if you've noticed such things.

I could recast my subhead as "the liberation of skiing," but that would make even more people mad at me than are going to be already. Do you see why? It would imply that skiing is presently enslaved somehow. ...A bad move for anyone who wants to interact with the industry!

Like everything, skiing is political. It doesn't stand alone. It's tied to culture in all sorts of ways. And its fate is tied to other sports. And it's tied to international commerce. The style of global trade in XC skiing – like the size of marketing budgets -- affects how we think of it, or don't.

What happens to a globally popular sport when it swings from having shops everywhere to having hardly any? What happens when a marketing strategy shifts from everyman to elite? I'll tell you what I think based on what it's like around me.

See how you think such notions relate to your scene. . . . Yeah, this is a different approach from your usual how-to hobby book.

In the US, class-status and our relationship to "health" comes into the story of winter fun. I'm going to unpack the silos for you (sorry, I kinda like that buzzphrase).

Yes, this is my own marketing attempt. But I'm trying to rely on reality since I don't have a budget. I'll show you what skiing can be aside from any cultural forces that are trying to boss you. Because with skiing nobody is the boss of you. There may be zero encouragement, zero local shops or classes, and no obvious place to go. At the same time, we've maybe heard that there's ski fun happening far away, or that a certain place and style is the ticket for the sweet action. I say forget what you think you know. If there's snow and you can get ahold of skis — then winter is yours. It's worked for me and my friends. I'll show you how.

XC is Winter's Skateboarding

With Nordic skiing, everywhere there's snow is your oyster.

Actually, why not just call it "skiing." Because that's what it is. Let's take control of this thing. Let other people name what they do. We ski. Other people do "liftserved skiing," or whatever they want to call it.

XC skiing is free. Free your heel and free your mind. If you want to add anything to it, feel free. Then you have to pay. That's where The Man comes in. Chairlifts and groomers belong to The Man. Snowboarding and The Man are all well and good, but there are reasons for skateboarding and free fun. Liberation and freedom are things, too. Disintermediate now!

Friluftsliv!

The wide range of ways we can have winter fun are not islands to themselves. XC is part of the democracy of winter fresh air. It's a cheap, sustainable activity that exploits nobody nor puts anybody up or down. Sure, other things are like this, too – conviviality is a good club to be in. The focus: LIFE.

XC can include any amount of community and friendship. You can do it alone or with people. You can go to the store. You can race it. You can explore with it. You can do a tricky little course. You can picnic with it. It keeps you warm when it's cold. You can do it around a bonfire or a sauna or hot tub. You can do it with apple juice or with white wine. It makes any good food taste better -- on the trail or before or after. It can go with camping, canoeing, ice-fishing or hunting. It can be done in the city or country or wilderness. It can be done with anyone, young or old. You can pull people with it, you can push them. You can be their eyes for them if they're blind. You can ski with just your arms if that's what you have, or just your legs, depending.

The Scandinavians call it FRILUFTSLIV. Isn't that a neat word? ...The fresh air life.

It's also part of the Danish scene called "hygge" -- their culture of cozy. Winter is a time for reflection, for hearth and home, fireplaces, woodstoves, saunas and hot-tubs. Cuddling on couches. ...But to make those things feel as good as possible, get outside first! Get your daily fresh air before you snuggle up with that cup of hot mulled wine. It'll taste that much better!

The northern peoples have long known how to deal with the darkness of winter. And, yes, they suffer from it, too, at times. But they know it's critical to get out every day and catch what little sun there is. Abuse all lunch-hour privileges at this time of year -- and push for new ones!

It's interesting, too, to me that the Nordic concept of sport is "idraet" which seems to have a bigger meaning for them than to us. It includes character, which it also does for us, but with more humility, which is why it took awhile for them to agree to participating in a winter Olympics. They were against record-setting. Amateurism is also more built into the concept. As is civics and citizenship.

Maybe the nations who best knew how folks had to stick together to make it through an awfully long dark time of year have good insights about sport and conviviality and how achievement should be viewed.

(I've often wondered how skiing flourishes in regions where it's mostly dark all winter.)

How Do I Know This?

I come from Michigan, a most average of snow country states. Like a lot of the people who are still skiing today, I came of age in the 1970's when outdoor fun was at its peak. All the outdoor activities fit together for me. I worked at an outdoor shop and when December rolled around we had a line of people waiting to buy ski packages snaking through the store, up the stairs, across a balcony then down and outside and along the block like we were a blockbuster movie! Our savvy shop crew was helping our city have fun outside. It meant a lot to us. (A shop next door was

the first cafe in town and also the first to sell imported wines and cheeses. Yet another wonderful education!) Michigan had dozens of outdoor and ski shops. Today only a few remain. I experienced the boom...and the bust.

Bill Koch was my hero, and every other skier's hero, too. He was the first US XC skier to win an Olympic medal -- an awesome, quirky athlete. Even more importantly, he was the star of an awesome short ski movie set in the maple sugaring corn snow season of New England. This short film was a big part of why a lot of my generation caught ski fever. It was often playing on screens in outdoor shops.

My brother and I started XC in the 1970's from a spirit of adventure -- for zooming down hills and jumping like Bill Koch. For us XC was like regular skiing only we didn't have to drive far or pay. Obviously, anywhere there was snow, we could explore, glide, and find downhills.

Somehow I grew up with a love of rivers and streams even though all I had around me as a child were drainage ditches. I suppose this helps inspire a big imagination. We are a can-do people. And some of us will not be stopped.

Our school had the wonderful help of a local guy named Ron Bacon. He started the local outdoor recreation program and included winter sports on the roster. He also hosted annual winter camp-outs for ALL the 4th and 7th graders for about 30 years, teaching thousands of kids all sorts of snow skills. There was no summer skills camp. Why send every suburban kid to winter camp? I think it was to build confidence, respect, and imagination. Everyone I knew was so excited! I really had few skills before this. So I really appreciate what Ron did for me and all us kids. Sure, we all loved playing in the snow, but he gave us knowledge.

In my 20's I got into canoe and kayak racing, road-biking, mt-biking, running and triathlons. It seemed like all XC skiers did these things, too.

"Breaking Away" and Greg Lemond arrived for the 80's and inspired us during the summers. I started bike racing and saw that some fun local bike racers were also skiing, with gusto. They showed me a wonderfully technical trail where we chased each other around, hollering, being crazy.

Mike Walden, as coach of the Detroit Sports Club Wolverine cycling club, had us skiing every winter. One of the winningest teams for its size, he developed world champs, Olympic medalists, and a Tour de France racer. The club logo featured a wheel, skate and ski.

One of my motivators was/is kind of funny: girls!

I used to do hunting and fishing: no girls. Then I started skiing and biking: yes girls! In the early 80's women's lib was liberating outdoor sport. Young guys and gals were playing outside with no adult supervision.

Skiing is romantic -- as is all fresh air fun. Those who think its appeal is one-sided machismo don't know it.

I escaped the hinterlands and moved to Colorado to get in on the outdoor action. There I met European NCAA skiers. They showed me that even the fastest skiers could be fun.

Out west I experienced the development and takeover of skating first-hand. I was happily swallowed whole by the marvels of each new technique.

I did a lot of racing for 10 years, helped develop a team, even got sponsored and went to the Nationals.

I had graduated in Journalism and worked in outdoor sports magazine writing and editing. I was an early adopter in desktop publishing, computing and websites and internet sales. When I moved back to Michigan, I started a zine called Out Your Backdoor (and then website) because I sensed a disconnect between

the official outdoors and the real fun: my zine showed the real deal.

Then I experienced the revival of classic skiing, which was like the joy of re-meeting a long lost friend.

I started noticing introversion and decline in XC. I felt the aridity of shops closing, shrinking events, and few new skiers.

Waxing and base prep became trickier and more expensive, but without it you got left behind.

Then I discovered trail skiing and saw how much control even basic gear now offers. I didn't need tracks anymore!

It's been so much fun being an early adopter all over again!

My friends and I now have so much fun even in low snow conditions.

Our casual trail skiing events have dozens of mt-bikers show up to ski the sweet singletrack, but so far only a couple "real" Nordic skiers. Ironic.

Our gang realizes that Nordic skiing has a "roadie" aspect that is overlooking trail skiing and the "mt-bike of skis."

Ten years of hosting "ski party" events show us their potential -- especially in low-snow conditions where "real" ski events are cancelled or reduced on the

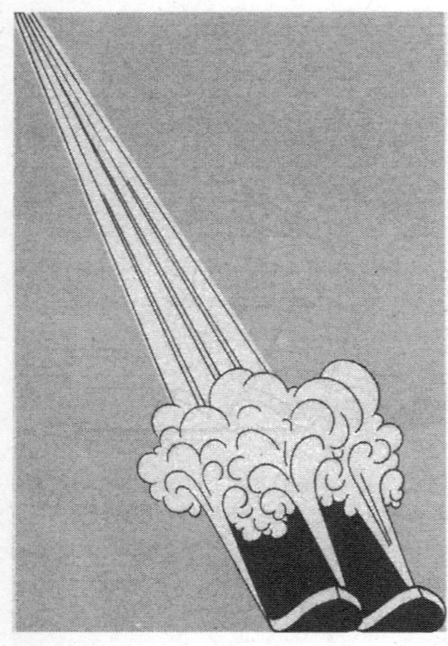

same days we are still romping in shady snow-holding forests.

Snowbike fever has diluted this a bit, but the thrill of singletrack skiing is holding!

We've also noticed mt-biking and road riding fading due to increased "seriousness." To offset this we started hosting casual, convivial bike events and feel a little spark coming back. I started co-hosting a popular urban "bike party" in our town after I saw social biking being a nationwide winner for diversity, inclusion, creativity, affordability... and awesome fresh air fun. I also saw the friendly gung-ho American approach to cyclocross take off.

I started teaching private and group XC lessons. And I've made a series of how-to videos on YouTube for my OutYourBackdoor channel. They seem to be popular! 400k views! It's satisfying to help people get a feel for skiing.

My friends and I study skiing, sharing and testing our observations. I've read the books and studied the videos. Everybody learns differently, but I've tried to detect which approaches are easiest for people to apply -- with no wasted or boring motions or distracting ideas.

I've seen in skiing that there's a big but invisible mid-section that gets pigeon-holed as "duffers" with the reputation for "knowing what they're doing" going to a small group that only goes for speed in one situation.

My friends and I have learned to party the snow that we do get here at an intensity beyond what the existing scene and industry can imagine. And we want to share the wealth.

I'm used to our culture being wrong about little things, but it's also bad with big things. Michigan is largely an unhealthy state. We rank low in all the fresh-air ways. Probably much of snow country is in the same boat.

Playing outside year-round is the only cure.

Nobody can afford to look down on whole months of the year. Being idle for even a few months each year starts a downhill slide that the rest of the year can't recover from -- and doesn't for most of our residents.

As a Michigander I hear the social rejection of winter daily and the reason I promote winter is that I'm not crazy. The more you move the warmer you are. And playing outside with your friends in what little winter sun we get has to be the best cure for winter depression. ...Science and logic are our friends.

Active life is subject to a lot of disconnects and negativity from a sickly general public. (Bikers know this the most.) My experiences have helped me empathize with other oppression in the US. ...The enemies of sustainability are interconnected.

Raising awareness is the answer! This book is my attempt to give a fresh boost to XC and winter. ...*Ride the wave!*

Ski Party: A Casual Party Tour

The Stinchfield Loppet is our picnic tour, the first in our annual series of Back-country Ski Parties. Our series has "one of each," including: a picnic tour; an intensely technical raid sort of race; a powder glades BBQ; a party relay; an out-n-back; and a daylong season-finale spring-ski epic. Each of our outings has something different to offer. ("Loppet" is Norge for long distance outing over varied terrain, usually skiing.)

We were nervous before the Stinchfield Loppet this one year. We had a 10" base, but a couple days with a forecast of 40 degrees leading into the event and 50+ for the day-of… Whew! What's THAT going to be like?

Well, weren't we surprised! The sun came out. And so did our t-shirts and shorts. We had a blast! Our skis worked great! The kickin' and glidin' didn't let us down. The shady forest at Stinch holds snow better than anywhere around.

Stinchfield Woods has the biggest hills for 100 miles around, pegging the meter for challenge and scenery. It's home for the U of M observatory on top of Peach Mountain. (We like to say we're skiers of the Peach Mountain Division.) I always

have to note that hardly any local hardcore XC skiers use these trails. Mt-bikers seem to "get" its ski appeal, though. Even though most skiers are also mt-bikers, the skiers just don't get it. Weird!

A big part of our style is outdoor antics with a cultural twist – we say that max food goes with Max VO2. But I think I need to bring along a better quality white wine. It's important. Sure, it's worth spending money on carbon poles and fluoro waxes, but don't forget quality with your wine.

I hope that people didn't mind my fannypack boombox. It could be like a Bike Party where if you don't like the tunes you

just drift further back or go off the front. (Bike Parties often have multiple music "clubs" so riders can pick the vibes they like.)

25 skiers showed up -- that's a lot of faith! We skied for a couple hours of no-drop fun for over 8 miles. I like our style of hilltop wait-ups. We cruise, then hammer the climbs, then hang out a bit.

We stayed together really well. It might be nice to create an alt-route to point a B Group to, to better match their druthers, and which ends up at the same picnic spots.

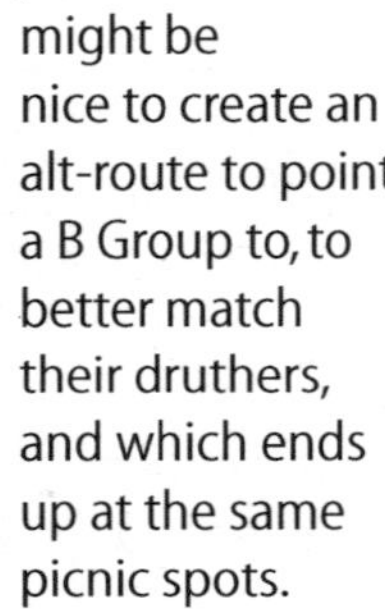

I think fluoro waxes are dandy for touring. Fluoros repel water from your bases bigtime. Racers aren't the only folks who love fast skis that work great! You don't need it all the time, but if it's gonna be sticky you can turn skis into rockets by crayoning it on. So what if it's expensive. It's not like we use it every day. My little cube has lasted for years.

Get out your rillers, too! This also breaks up the suction of wet snow. I've often used a file held on edge.

We took breaks at scenic overlooks. Nuthin' wrong with standing around chatting in the sun and 45 degrees!

Stinch has 7 or 8 hills about a half-mile long – winding, with changing pitches. Awesome going up or down. With names like Rollercoaster and Corkscrew what's not to love! (The local "serious" skiers shun Stinch because, they say, they don't have "rock skis" or tour skis. I say: go get some. So you can *get some*.)

As the day warmed we enjoyed translucent snow with oak leaves floating in it. Picturesque bliss to us. We almost had flowing water in the trail at one point: Peach River!

We had a mid-trail picnic at the halfway point. Then we did our usual parking lot potluck afterward. All good!

We're lucky to have Dave... Once after a Loppet he missed he pulled into the lot, did a power-U, dropped his tail-gate and unveiled a steaming batch of fresh buffalo wings. ...Food and party skiing go together!

Culture: The Nordic Experience

What is skiing like, anyway? I've read a lot of descriptions of it, many saying that it's a "great workout." But that's like saying sex is for fitness. *Ahem...* Or like dancing is for cardio.

There's an old hippie saying that deserves a revival: "Free the heel, free the mind."

Skiing is like dancing over hill and dale. It's like ice-skating over the countryside in hilly terrain.

It's all-body action with 4 sticks and basically no moving parts.

Skiing has a rhythmic range of motion ... and the more varied the terrain and the more trail-like of a place you're skiing, the more expressive and diverse will be your dynamic range.

Skiing is One. No matter what kind of skis are on our feet, we assume the Ready Stance and keep a forward posture. The kind of skiing we do is simply determined by the terrain we're in.

Skiing is a great way to experience in winter the same trails that you enjoy biking in summer. ... Except you use a wider range of motion and less equipment. It's great cross-training that breaks you break out of the linearity of bike-motion where hands, butt, feet are restricted by the limits and angles of the bike-frame and drivetrain. It's low impact like biking but weight-bearing like running ... plus the armwork.

In snowy winter our same-old trails come back to life new for us. Possibly we're a little tired of their green selves. Thankfully a world of four seasons keeps offering us fresh views! In winter our trails offer all-new vistas because the leaves are down -- the forests have opened up. Now we can see so far! The air is refreshingly cleaner.

The Blue Hour

Have you heard of the Blue Hour? Take up skiing and find yourself relishing that special time of day. It happens for a mysterious amount of time after sunset and before dark. You can still see to ski -- but it would be smart to wear your headlamp because soon it'll be dark. But the blue, the blue... Those who play outside on snow

Look out your door. ...Play that way. Ski the most in the way that's easiest. Ski or play the other ways for a special treat or while on a trip.

They say "If you can walk you can ski." I raise the bar: "If you can DANCE you can ski!"

My three reasons for snow fun really seem to cover it all. None can be removed. And there's no reason to add to them. Whattaya think? Once again:

GLIDE.

RHYTHM.

FLOW.

As long as we have these 3, we smile.

Glide: Sometimes people say they like a sport because "it's fast." Well, c'mon, speed is relative. Why do we like speed? Downhill skiing is generally faster than XC but then XC gear and clothing is lighter which offsets the raw numbers. I mean, a car is faster than any skiing but it's so armored that it doesn't give us a feeling of speed.

Rhythm: It's tempo and beat -- the pattern of turning or striding, weighting and unweighting. If it's steady and in harmony with the terrain and the design of the equipment then it brings smiles. We can get all the rhythm we need from any kind of skiing -- if there's no rhythm you're not really doing it.

in winter get to enjoy this subtle evening glow. I wouldn't miss it for anything.

When did you last go out and play in the snow under a full moon and clear sky? ...You could even read outside then. It's a good time to ski. Try it.

Why is Snowsport Fun?

My mantra is that the keys to winter fun are: Glide, rhythm, flow. Also: all snowsport is One.

I want to be the Dr. Bronner of winter fun! (He's the hippie soap guy.)

Snowboarding, downhill, skating, striding, telemark... you name it. Ice-skating and snowshoeing even! It's all fun for the same basic reasons!

Why do one instead of another? As far as I can tell the only reason to pick one kind of snow fun over another is when it's CLOSER and more sustainable and that fits our conditions and weather the best. And which can give you the most all-body health and fitness.

So, ski the one that brung ya.

Flow: That's our payoff. When the effort we're making feels worthwhile: when it feels like we're getting more back than we're putting in, that's flow. You're doing some work but you're also getting glide with a nice rhythm so it strikes you viscerally as being worth it. Gliding or linking turns down a hill is payoff. But you don't want to feel like you worked too hard getting up the hill. Nor do you want to work too hard getting down it while staying upright, either. When something has a positive work vs reward ratio we have flow. When any output feels like more than the input, you'll have a grin. Uphills are actually where one can feel a lot of payoff because it's where one can easily feel so little. When you feel like you're gliding easily up a hill with a nice rhythm your payoff factor can feel, like, three times better than if you're laboring. Gliding down a hill tends to give easy payoff to everyone (until tricky conditions and turns come into the picture).

Scenery is a factor, too. The nice thing about winter is that it puts a whole new look on everywhere we've gotten so used to seeing the rest of the year. Our local forests and waterways look entirely different. Getting out into a fresh winter landscape gives a scenic thrill.

In the end, fun is about ***people***. No skier is an island. When we play together in the snow then no matter what we do we have fun. The way to judge the best snowsport in this case would seem to be the way of playing that's easiest for folks to get into. And the widest variety of folks is best of all. Modes that are more restrictive or refined can be saved for special occasions, like expeditions or extreme attempts.

The Way It Was

XC ramped up, built and grew through the 1970's just before I came of age at its frenzied peak in the USA. I missed the build-up and its main style. XC was really a thing when Mother Earth News was big and the Whole Earth Catalog was even bigger.

For the whole ramp up, XC was distinguished by a mellow rasta style. Wood skis and wool. 60-40 parkas. Cotton killed, but jeans were fine if nobody noticed. Bota bags, grass and saunas.

Do you know what a bota bag is? It's a wineskin. The hippies and everyone in Europe used to go on winter outings and always bring a bota bag of white wine or apple juice. (I say let's "Bring Back the Bota Bag." Sling it over your shoulder, tuck it inside if need be so it doesn't freeze. Bring a picnic, too.)

Then came fiberglass skis and soon to follow was brightly colored synthetic fabric and plastic bindings. XC was still rocking when shiny lycra bodysuits splashed on the scene and bewildered everybody.

Using those skis was akin to surfing. Control was tenuous and was gained through technique and vibes. They had to be finessed. They often weighed a fair bit and had a mind of their own. The boots were soft and usually low-cut and were used to make subtle suggestions to the skis. Grooming hardly existed! After a few years a major local race might have a snowmobile and a single track after a race got into the woods. Doubleset tracks only appeared after a decade of growth and frustration. Passing had a strong etiquette but was problematic. "Track!"

Hundreds of people clamored to race or ski "loppet" tours in multiple events each weekend in each local area throughout our region.

Hundreds of new Nordic trail systems materialized anywhere a community found a scenic chunk of land. Trail pride was a thing.

XC ski shops popped up in almost every snow country college or mountain town.

Performance was had thanks to pine-tar, hardwax and klister, all of which had leaned on Lore, if not voodoo. "What should I use?" ...You used what someone you heard knew how to do it said to use.

John Caldwell's book came out and sold jillions of copies. It had artfully evocative photos that vaguely hinted at how to ski. It advised in the fall to start chopping wood and pulling on bicycle inner tubes hung from trees and doing hill-bounding. So we did.

Imagination was a big part of it.

So was the Ski Pro. Alpine had sexy instructors on every hill. XC had them, too, in every community recreation catalog.

Skis frequently BROKE. Where racing skis could be found they broke even more often. People carried a plastic spare ski tip even on casual outings. (Our local club placed a group order for racing skis once a year.)

Bamboo poles were tough (and still work quite well).

Gaiters were everywhere. Often home-made.

Military surplus was frequently called back into service.

The wood skis felt good in soft snow. ...And they still do.

Nobody knew what training was. The word "interval" was occasionally uttered as the ski-boom entered its middle years.

Guys and gals wanted an outdoor winter challenge and they wanted to be outside together without meddling oversight.

XC fit right in with the backpacking craze that was hitting during the summer. Canoeing was also booming. Biking of all kinds was huge. Equipment for any sport was simple but at the premium levels offered elite crafts-

manship.

Telemark turns were dabbled in using the same set of gear used for all your other skiing.

Then everything got better and better and better. And skiing got serious. Then skating showed up. Then winters became sketchy. And ski culture went topsy-turvy, with a few hotspots growing and every-where else dropping way off. And here we are.

The Way It is Now

The public now experiences winter and outdoor sport in a lot of different ways since the days when skiing was the winter fun of choice, and since the last innova-tions in XC skiing equipment, technique or instruction. These changes hugely affect how people perceive skiing.

Within skiing itself the biggest change in recent decades is the establishing of elite technology in the preparing of skis. The thrill of successful ski selection, flex choice, base prep and waxing is esoteric beyond compare, but it's real. Its potential market for enthusiasts is microscopic: it's like finding the crossover demographic between microscope scientists and 100-yard dash sprinters.

Prepping a ski so that it glides like a miracle device on a highly prepped snow surface is indeed thrilling. Talk about the pay-off feeling. With perfect skis it feels like you're riding a silent and, um, invisible snowmobile. Actually, ski prep doesn't have to be complex, but it does take some time and money to make fun skis.

Thus the aspect that has come to be most influential in the not-surprisingly shrinking world of US XC skiing is a laboratory-like workshop, complete with respirator, since the substances used are toxic.

I felt alienated by this chemistry aspect. I felt the shock the most the one time that I clearly had the fastest wax. It seemed like cheating.

Then I discovered the thrill of skiing challenging local hiking trails. I told my ski racing friends but none were inter-ested. A ski shop owner suggested I get in touch with a hardcore mt-biking skier named RadNord who lived near me. He was surprised we hadn't yet met. So I contacted him and told him I was hosting a ski event on a challenging hiking trail. He told me about one that he had started not long before, on the most extreme local mt-biking trail. I showed up to his event and was impressed by the gathering of gungho outdoor people. When I saw how they were equipped, my heart melted. I never saw such motley gear! Mis-matched poles and duct-taped boots. This gang was out to ski a crazy trail and to have fun. I'd never seen a ski race where people brought a BBQ grill to the parking lot, or built a bonfire next to the cars, or pulled out 6-packs. These people were enjoying themselves on the weekend. Skiing was a time to kick back and have a hoot. . . . And to use whatever gear worked. They didn't want skis that glided fast. They wanted to glide SLOWER because they were on a steep, narrow, twisty trail where control was more important than speed.

To me, these guys and gals represented the mt-biking of skiing. . . . And the future of skiing. Just as the mt-bike blew up biking. But nobody knew it before it hit. And few know now about the potential for XC. ...But the scene is ripe for the New Wave!

Skiing On the Screen

The biggest opportunity to hit skiing overall was the advent of the Internet. The public can now more easily learn about XC skiing than ever before. Thanks to YouTube we can learn so much about skiing variety and heritage. But for viewing the modern era, we can see anything as long as it's about groomed ski racing — except for my homestyle OYB videos! So, we can dig deeper and find traces of the old ways.

This is a vast improvement from before the Net when the sport, which is nearly uncoached in the US, had very little help available in person or video. I remember getting ahold of rare Norwegian VHS technique tapes. Our nation's whole tiny world of XC skiers experienced ski technique breakthroughs, thanks to those tapes, a few technique clinics, and one magazine -- bringing skills refined overseas.

Heritage footage is freely available. We can see how skiers played and raced in any previous era. We can watch training videos for WW2's 10th Mountain Division, or the earliest recorded footage from the mountains of Eastern Europe.

Fasterskier.com, the only Nordic news site, is dedicated to groomed FIS track racing. The only discussion forum, xcskiforum. com, is enjoyed globally -- by a handful. The several mail order catalogs have websites and continue to do their best but focus on groomed trail racing. Info on the magic of elite waxing is shared by several gurus and sales reps like Zach Caldwell on Caldwellsport.com as well as the gang from Boulder Nordic Sport – a wonderful rabbit hole to disappear down.

Ski media is divided into groomed skiing and Big Air powder mountain backcountry skiing. The two worlds do not overlap nor do they acknowledge a middle ground.

How do Snowbikers See Skiing?

Today, when outdoor buffs notice XC skiing for the first time their snow experience may well have been shaped by a snowbike.

In light of the experience of snowbiking, how might someone perceive XC skiing? I've discussed aspects of this already, but let's dig in further. I would think bikers could see skiing as biking liberated. Suddenly you have no gear to speak of (no moving parts), and a free range of motion. You get propulsion from every part of your body. As you work in rhythm each part of you contributes to the flow. You're just standing poised on simple, flat things, gathering up then expanding, coiling then pouncing -- gently, with no impact.

Bikers like to cross-train for health and results. Skiing is ideal snow-time training to get the body out of a fixed-motion pedaling rut while still working bike-ish muscles and energy systems. Win-win! (Speed-skating has also been used as north-country cross-training for bikers, but I don't know its popularity lately.)

Those who already love skiing often add a snowbike to their fleet and find that the sports mix fine – they use the fatbike to enjoy marginal conditions common in climate-change -- then switch to skis once the glide comes on.

Snowbikers at least are loving winter, but soft snow and powder days are their point of vulnerability: here bikes flounder but skis win easily. ...Especially for earning turns in the BC.

But due to today's recreation segregation, bikers often don't know enough about XC skiing to form an opinion and there's nobody around, few retail shops, to clue them in.

Today Zwift and other smart trainers have made it even easier to pedal when conditions aren't right for fattying. Yeah, they say it's fun, but...c'mon.

I think bikers want to experience seasonal variety as much as anyone. It's a desire regardless of whether you have seasons where you live or you choose to go where the climate is different. And for people desiring a change of pace it's natural to change the activity at least some of the time.

The Range of Fun on Skis

What is the variety of action we can have in a day on skis? Let's see…

First, location...We can ski on ski trails. We can also enjoy glide-flowing the same trails we loved biking and hiking on all summer. We can also ski anywhere else there's snow: meaning all sorts of places we do NOT go in summer: we can now walk on water! We can fly over hill and dale WITHOUT trails.

Here's a list of possible fun that stretches

A whole generation of funhogs was inspired by champion Bill Koch and the short film he made back in the day. It showed him playing in the snow and picnicking with friends. It's time for a new wave of fun!

way out, and it's all actually pretty simple with low overhead:

Stride touring, fast classic, skate-skiing, crust skiing classic, crust skate-skiing, skiing on hiking and mt-biking trails, groomed courses, or frozen waterways, skiing in the cold on packed powder, skiing when it's warm on juicy corn, skiing on thin snow, on slush, on ice, ice skates for when it's cold and dry, fast sprints on short loops, marathon events, pursuit races or outings where you ski both classic and skate in one day or weekend, citizen racing, biathlon events or setting a bb-gun out on a picnic table and skiing loops around your yard stopping each lap to shoot at pop-cans dangling from tree-limbs, Nordix/Nordicross where you ski technical courses, trail laps around a bonfire, near a picnic table laid with snacks, picnics on a trail, stopping for a snack on a log halfway through an outing, workouts, campouts on overlooks, romping with little kids and families, hauling a pulk full of kids or gear, renting rentals, demo'ing

Here I am enjoying the Striding Doublepole, a versatile move not taught in any official material. Why is that? Skiing shouldn't limit itself.

warm and heavy, liftserved tele groomed or ungroomed, Alpine Touring where you clamp your heel down to power-descend then release it for the uptrack – this isn't distance striding but it's fun, so it's good, offseason tidying-up of your favorite local northfacing snowholding slopes and glades – moving dead brush to dial in fall-lines for winter. ...*Whew!*

What Makes Awesome?

To do a kind of skiing other than on the snow near you requires non-skiing. Like, driving or flying to the snow. Or working to get money to pay for access. I'd rather be skiing. So my advice is: Get thee to the closest snow! Add the rest as occasional special treats.

When I lived in the mountains in a ski resort town I got used to world-class skiing every day within a mile of home. I since moved back to Michigan I made friends with others who've skied a lot in the mountains. We all insist on world class quality.

It seems like the main value my hardcore gang cherishes is proximity. Having snow in or near your neighborhood is the best. Other values are important, too, but that's where it starts. So if you have that, be proud! And enjoy it! Your skis sure will!

The other main values our gang shares are the opportunities for flow trail and quality ski handling. Next is scenery and views. (The views don't need to be big-sky vistas. Ridges and waterways are just dandy.)

"Great" snow isn't that close to the top of our list. Because we know all snow is

fancy gear you haven't tried before, skiing-in first tracks on a casual trail, skiing where the whole neighborhood (including the dog-walkers) has already packed a firm tread, ski jumping from a wedge of snow kicked up onto the side of a hill, floating out into the air over the slope with your ski tips coming up on any old skis, just like on TV, skiing a tricky course laid out in a forest with banked turns and swoops up and down ravines, cyclocross style, light touring with a little telemark mixed in, BC skiing on middleweight gear with striding mixed with tele turns both in the trails and on the hillsides, BC skiing with heavier gear focusing on tele turns on a gladed slope or in a meadow, with relaxing uptracks taking you directly back up to the action, moving over a couple feet with every run, keeping an eye on the sun, changing valley sides when the snow gets too great. Still, when the big dumps roll in, we know what to do! …Hit the pow!

We know that when you get a lot of snow if you live anywhere near a hill you can shred it up as nicely as if you were in Aspen.

A day or so after a big pounding the trails will be skied-in enough to lure us back to the kick'n'glide.

Of course there's a time and place for the exotica of travel. Do it if you can when the time is right. But if you can't, no big deal. Skiing doesn't have anything to do with money or travel: it's about snow.

I now live in a place that has snow but isn't any sort of mecca. My friends and I have figured out how to find the mecca within.

Epic-ness is related to awesomeness. It's a world-class factor we search for, hunger for every year. Epic isn't necessarily an everyday experience, but it can be. Grandeur, largesse, intensity, and exploring limits relate to epic. But it's uncommon. Given our unpredictable weather we keep a constant eye out for epic conditions and we seize the day when they appear. It's a time to play hooky. It often means skiing a trail or a route that we seldom have enough snow to enjoy. It means going big for hours. It requires pushing and a mix of skillsets. Skiing from dark-to-dark is epic. But so can be grabbing a morning's worth of turns from a overnight dump of a foot of freshies on tidied-up glades.

The Quality of Trail

I note that hiking trails often deliver more scenery than do golf courses, which is where a lot of bland skiing defaults to. Golf courses in the winter aren't always bad, but often they are. Be picky. Usually golf courses allow casual winter visitation without the fee associated with their summer use. So you might as well go top shelf. The better courses have the better hills and scenery, don't they. Still, hiking trails are generally superior for scenery than either ski trails or golf courses.

But hiking trails aren't designed for ideal ski flow. Even so, many can be readily adapted, even on the fly, to this end. When a line doesn't suit you, just ski off the trail and sort out a line that does! BC skis are now designed to be so nimble today that you can do this on the fly. To make a trail you'll use again, it might require kicking aside some deadfall, but skiing is also awesome because casual trails can be laid out so easily. Mt-bikers love making trail but they have to work so hard at it! It requires so much more than just leaving tracks in the snow. …And once the snow melts the ski trail disappears. The ultimate in leave-no-trace.

Another aspect of world class is the designed trail. Ski trail design can be simple or it can involve budgets, manpower and bulldozers. In the winter, design is simplest of all: just ski the best lines for any given terrain. But to do this best involves work in the autumn. You find land you want to turn into world class skiing, land with varied topography. Maybe you've attempted to ski it already. But in the fall you look at it and see what needs to be done to make it world class. Generally all it needs is for you to move some deadfall. Make sure it's OK, but you might also want to prune non-

Back in the day a little ol' Detroit club had this logo … and they won world championships in biking and skating. Skiing played a big part in their success, and their fun.

desirable saplings and toss rocks aside. Then once the snow flies you can find yourself with just the route your heart desires, ready to be skied-in for world-class fun. And if you've done true tidying, picking up little sticks and pebbles, it can deliver with only a couple inches of snow.

Be Prepared – Use the Buddy System

As with all trails, read your map and bring it! Bring a headlight. Keep your phone warm, bring an external battery. Know where you're going. Look before you leap (especially with challenging downhills).

Use the buddy system: ski with a friend. For trails that are miles from the road or where you started, bring a repair kit and first aid.

Tracks in the Woods

Most skiing doesn't happen at specific resorts. It's done on just plain trails, in parks, and other accessible places with snow: fields, frozen waterways.

People usually ski-in their own routes. The first time after a snowfall is slow going. A day later that trail has set up and become firmer and faster. It gets more fun with every use.

These trails are often local favorites year-round. Skiers often have to share them with many other kinds of users, including fatbikes.

Here is an awesome aspect of home-made ski trails in contrast from machine-groomed trails. Figure skating used to be known by the *marks* it made on the ice. And elite alpine skiing is sometimes highlighted by perfectly linked figure-8 tracks as people ski runs across a pristine hillside then look back and admire their handiwork. Well, XC skiing has this, too. Everyday casual skiers know it well, but nobody has put it into words that I've seen. When we ski-in our own loops we leave specific marks. The quirks of our strides leave their traces. Most of our turns are flowing tangents, sometimes leaving only one line as we stride each ski around a bend, changing direction with each glide. If a trail is skied in one direction these marks develop a pleasing visual character, especially if it's just you skiing the route. Your style leaves its mark. As you round each turn, you'll tend to make the same moves. However, if people start skiing it in both directions the distinct look of the trail can fade. And different skiers can have totally different ways of handling a situation, leaving different marks. Enjoying our traces is yet another fun part of XC.

We can even identify each other by our marks! They give hints on the skill and fitness of the skier. (Pole marks far apart mean the skier was going fast.) Nowax skis also leave a pattern from their gripzone.

…With machine-grooming we rarely see special marks. A uniform set of grooves encourages everybody to keep their skis in place.

Then there's the coolness of just plain tracks in the snow. Snow tracks tell the stories of everyone and every-thing that has passed that way. People who play in the snow get to enjoy all this!

I appreciated seeing the tracks of an otter in snow just a few hours old, romping down a local frozen river I was skiing on. I didn't know otters were around here! They are shy, but they leave tracks in the snow! I saw how it danced a big circle with a coyote then interacted with a couple raccoons at a place where the river wasn't frozen and animals were gath-ering by the flowing water.

The Thrill of the White

One of the unique and awesome de-lights of XC skiing are the occasions when we get lost in the white. For me this hap-pens on wide open trail in big sky country, with trees off to the sides, out of the pic-ture, out of my view. It happens in the best way possible on big outings. Really, it's one of the miracles of long distance skiing. A marathon will do. It impresses one specifi-cally with classic striding. What I mean is: the back and forth of colorful skis on white snow. Watching the skis go forward and back. Over and over again. With white below and white beyond and everywhere in your periphery. It still works if a skier is ahead of you and their skis are also going back and forth in your view. It is the quin-tessence of being mesmerized. With skate-skiing the skis are leaving your field of attention off to the left and right. They're not even really in your thoughts. You just look at the trail ahead. As if you were running. But with striding you see your skis. ...Back and forth. If you're skiing in unbroken snow you might only see the tips breaking through...back and forth. It's easy to lose the horizon. It can even be disorienting. You can lose yourself. It's not in any other situations in life where we find ourselves gliding across fields of white. ...Enjoy.

The Joy of Cold

I'm thinking the most common winter situation today is a slightly hilly town that gets some snow but is slushier than it used to be. The folks who live there are people who might want to look into what it might mean to have fun in the

snow with friends, with kids, and even to do it until the day they die, like people have done for millennia. But nowadays cold seems daunting. Such towns have retreated from winter but aren't that much warmer. …It hurts whenever you're hustling between shelter and car. Yet folks there don't play outside as much as they used to.

Cold schmold… it's just so relative. Cold-hearted is the only thing we have to worry about. Winter isn't cold! You're active as always, you wear clothes, you're warm. You're not cold. Cold sounds inhospitable, yet winter is obviously a time for romping, for hugging, for being invigorated!

Today's advances in technology in clothes and in gear serve people so well and so affordably. Old stuff works great, too.

Once it's winter the main thing is to keep playing outside. Snow and cold are your friends. Colors are brighter, air is cleaner, vistas wider. If you like doing things outside in the summer, you're good for winter, too. Really, you need to! For your health, sanity and just plain fun!

And snow is around well into spring in many places. Snow can be warm and sunny. It's part of flowing creeks and returning birdies.

The human body moving around does a great job of creating warmth. If you're moving you won't be getting cold. Put on some layers to keep the wind off of you but prevent heat or sweat from building up and you're all set. Then go find the pretty places. Once it snows they're almost everywhere! (More on staying warm later.)

Slow down and simplify in the dark winter, if you like. Cozy is king! Make fires in fireplaces. Take more saunas. Snuggle up. Google "hygge" and discover how the Danes do winter coziness. … But also get outside! The cozy is then that much better! They're not kidding when they say that winter darkness can be a bummer. …Especially if you live in a gray climate. Some places are sunny in winter. Others aren't. You need to get fresh air and at least a little sunshine every day!

Once it's spring, get out there for the face tans and the even-fresher snow-melt air.

I highly recommend sorting out a revised lunch-hour routine for winters. Before and after work it's often dark. Liber-ate lunch-time and get outside! Cheat a bit and snack before and after. It's better to skip lunch in winter than it is to skip the little daylight we get during the week.

Like Antonina Anikin, the famous Olym-pic ski coach, says: "Old Russian saying -- Summer is good for the heart. Winter is best for the soul."

Of course, if dark is all you get, make hay. Back when skiing was 5X popular people still had jobs and it still got dark in winter. ...And they didn't have common headlamps! Our winter lighting scene today is so much better than it was during the Ski Boom. (I got one of the first headlamps. My friend couldn't afford one so we'd both go skiing after work by the pale yellow light of my light. Once he didn't see a low tree branch in time...)

A lot of big parks and wild areas are miles from town. In town we see more compact parks and skiing opportunities. In our city we've laid out a couple world-class singletrack flow loops that give sublime ski experience in small, sheltered settings.

A nice thing about cities is there's cozy nearby. Each of our city park trails has a pub on its perimeter or within a few blocks. We call them our ski lodges. We ski right up and make a grand entrance and enjoy a cozy apres' ski scene of our own making. We can't help but come in with gusto and cold air sticking to us (I'm guessing these are friendly negative ions), especially if it's night and we've been skiing with our headlamps. It's a good way to order a beer.

I know there are a few people who are "allergic" to the cold, who have "conditions." These folks should resist with all their might and resourcefulness having these ailments hold them back. (I suppose most of them do resist! Why wouldn't they? Yes, there's Raynaud's Syndrome. But for the 4% who have it, figure out a workaround!)

Do your hands and feet get cold? Work your butt off figuring out when and how and if there is any situation in which your results change. Is your issue simplistic or complex? In my own case, my extremities wander and swing between warm and cold in all sorts of ways, many mysterious. I'll go out and soon my hands will be frozen but then they always make a comeback, though even then they go through a couple different phases. There are equipment solutions: mittens and thicker socks, chemical heat pouches with their miraculous dose of iron powder.

Singletrack Fever

Mt-biking has its famous singletrack jones. Much less well-known is that XC skiing has it, too. It's just not covered in the media or groomed-for at official XC resorts. XC actually beats out the mt-bike: when threading a narrow course. Because on skis you can pivot on a heel rather than having to guide a whole bike.

So where do you find tasty XC single-

Parking lot apres' ski parties are where it's at. A fire-pan is a good idea (maybe made from an old small-car hood?), but whatever works...

track? Just hit any of your fave mtb or hiking singletrack when the snow flies! It's not likely to be groomed, so ski it in yourself and use touring skis. Groomed ski trails are usually too wide and too tame to give the singletrack dyno thrill. Our motto is:"Ski what you ride."

You don't even need a trail at all. You can just make your own---find a fun route through the snowy woods and ski it in a few times. Instant trail! No enviro impact.

After winter, it's gone with the snow.

Trails come in all flavors. But if you want a thrill, that can be arranged!

Bill Koch recently complained in a "Cross Country Skier" mag interview that handling skills aren't pushed these days in XC, even on the World Cup level. I agree, though I suspect that skiing a WC course would still be a huge thrill! (I've read they're hard for many athletes even to walk around.) Before litigation-fear really

sank in (it first hit in the early 80's when XC tried to take off) an expert-level groomed trail could be wild and challenging indeed. These trails have since been greatly smoothed, taking away the thrill and the imaginary lawsuit risk (why not just have a double-diamond grade so you can say they were warned). You basically have to track-in thrilling trails yourself now.

To look at handling skills further, with XC you're using the whole body and ideally use full abandonment as you throw yourself into the moves. You blast corners, catch air, your limbs tossed every which way by G-forces. You're chest-first to the elements, flying down the hills, twisting the chutes, upright and exposed.

With singletrack in particular, you're doing snaky body moves, sometimes pivoting your skis from edge to edge in a single move. Striding smoothly thru tight turns is an art: you don't have to skate or skid all turns, you can stride them by swinging your outside tail wide and timing pole-plants with whatever tree you're dodging. Sometimes we leave only one ski down as we stride gliding from curve to curve.

And, as with figure skating, the marks we leave can be part of the artful fun. I enjoy skiing a tricky route over and over using the same strides, adding no extra marks. ...Especially when only one ski is down at a time.

A dropping whoop-de-doo section of singletrack is amazing. Your little trail sends you flying over hummocks as you go down, down, turning left, right, with prejumps coming at you, catching air here and there, sometimes barely keeping a ski on the ground to make the next turn. No need for a smooth straight downhill in the singletrack scene! (And no singletracker would ever design a hard turn at the bottom of a hill like so many lame ski course designers have done. When you work small, you can work right! I suppose many designers in the past included old logging two-tracks in their layouts so that groomers could easily fit through.)

Singletrack XC gets you close to the scenery. With XC equipment you're so free that it's no problem to line a trail right between majestic trees, or so close to them that you have to drop a shoulder to miss em. It's easy to squat low to get under an overhanging limb, or jump a log, or even ski up and over one. You can even run down a frozen creek, thru cattails and over a swamp or lake and back up into the trees. No worry about wide, heavy grooming machines here!

XC offers a wide range of action. Everything on your bod is swinging and flinging far and wide. Yet it's so easy to time it all with obstacles. You can be rocketing along on one foot, chin out, shimmying thru the trees.

XC is also like swing dancing! (I've been learning swing lately.) The arm action in telemark seems particularly Charleston-esque! Keeping your Big Mo flowing through singletrack involves seamlessly changing up between all techniques, sometimes using a different move on each stroke, all in rhythm. In fact, in other languages the skating moves have names like "paddle dance" and "double dance." XC has a beat!

Discovery awaits those who play in the snow. (After the first warm night of the year, the sallies can come out ... even with a lot of snow on the ground.)

The smaller the trail the more the intimacy. So if we really want to build up our quality social time for on-trail hanging out, visiting and bumping shoulders, singletrack is a sweetspot.

Springtime brings sunny melts and refreezes. Crust happens the morning after a freeze and is for skiing or skating anywhere in the woods, dodging trees, flying over the lakes, leaping the fields, having a blast. It's total liberation. It's singletrack everywhere! ...Or maybe it's wide open highway skiing everywhere? How about both!

Singletrack amplifies the thrill of any given terrain. It also steps up the required skill level. Take it easy when first skiing any new trail, especially one that wasn't designed for skiing. Mellow hiking and mt-bike singletrack can easily require expert level skills on skis. Scout downhills and don't hesitate to walk down them first to inspect then walk back up partway and take a couple tries as you get to get to know them on skis.

It's known that forests and mt-bike trails are cool in summer---compared to the parching heat of pavement. It's less known that woods are warm in winter. Moreover, the littler the trail, and the closer the trees, the warmer and cozier you'll be. Plus your snow can last weeks longer in the shade.

Singletrack culture also has good looking fashion. Such skiers probably aren't on a race team nor going all-out for aerodynamics, so they have the latitude to put together free-spirited outfits.

XC in general makes every part of you strong, flexible and longlasting. But a skier who moves around dynamically on narrow trails is better prepared when weird things happen, like tweaks or crashes, and is less apt to get hurt or strained.

Remember that casual singletrack trails can be basically "leave no trace." All it takes is a little vision as you cruise the terrain to see where a trail wants to be, to optimize flow, fun and handling skills. Then either just ski it in, or do a little pruning and dead-limb tossing first. (Of course, use common sense and conform to local regs.) You can often lay out new singletrack at a strolling pace. Come the springtime melt it's like no one was ever there. With XC singletrack there's no erosion. You're just lining up the lines and moving snags from underfoot, nothing more. It's fast, easy, low impact. (Bust out into fields or onto frozen waterways now and then to give a freaky change of pace and some big sky.)

As for singletrack gear, consider that narrow, noodly race skis at 44mm wide are designed for tracks, though you can "under-ski" them! (It's just like under-biking!) A ski that's a bit wider, 48-52mm, covers a wider range yet is still glide-oriented. An all-terrain ski of, say, 58mm gives more stabilty in ungroomed snow -- and more glide there, too -- yet still works fine in set-tracks, and is more potent for power-turns. Such skis are strong, too. I do jumps, and use em as bridges, no problem. Now add the recent mid-length concept to the mix to boost the handling!

The new "mt-bike of skis" kit is truly the cat's meow on singletrack: midlength wide-ish skis, cuffed boots and strong bindings give easy control on technical trails.

MTB goes MTXC! The concepts are parallel: For even more control you can add metal edges and go wider and wider, getting more float and control/turn power as your desired terrain gets steeper. You can beef up the boots stepwise, too. And bindings. Yet these rigs still have nice glide! And most have a nowax gripzone!

A midlength ski that's 80-100mm wide with a stout boot and BC binding lets you stride and pop tele turns as you please! Talk about free-ride!

At any pace, for scenery and an all-body workout and the rewards of handling skills and technique transitions, try XC singletrack!

Care of Casual Snowtrails

Many trails are groomed simply by skiing them in or being packed by enough walkers. After a few times being skied, and some cold overnight hours to set up, any trail becomes wonderful for skiing.

A trail used by a dozen or more classic skiers doesn't need any machinery to become nice to ski. However, fresh snow is needed each week to keep it nice. If conditions are dry too long it becomes icy and harsh and requires metal edges for control.

By contrast, skate-skiing requires machine grooming to deliver a good experience on a good course. DIY grooming is possible but would never be preferred. Yet a skied-in classic trail can provide an experience superior to machine grooming, especially in terms of scenic value, but also more interesting and challenging skiing.

When a trail is regularly used by quite a few walkers after any modest snowfall it also will tend to be pleasant to ski on even though it doesn't have set-tracks. Our "mt-bike of skis" gives enough control that you can ski relaxed even without tracks.

When sharing trails with walkers try to work with them via management and signs to train them to not walk on established ski tracks. Signs might need to be posted right in the trail at the trailhead. During freeze/thaw cycles trails should maybe be closed to all users at certain times to avoid huge splashy postholes that then freeze and hamper everyone. It only takes one walker in bad conditions to mess things up for days. "Do no harm" is a good motto for the trail community. Snowbikers seem to be the leaders in mixed-use snowtrail care at this point.

Machine grooming supports the most traffic and can manage both a lot of snowfall and revive icy trails if there's less snow.

But if there's low overall snowfall most

resorts won't groom, even though in shady forests there can be enough snow for classic skiing.

When an area is seeing only slight snowfalls or maybe freezing rain on a frozen trail bed then fatbiking might be the only realistic mode for flow fun.

Extra heavy snowfall can be too much of a good thing for skiers (and snowbikers, too). This also usually happens a few times each season. Machine grooming can quickly catch back up, but homestyle trail-making can leave skiers wallowing for days as fresh snow keeps falling. The solution is: friends, and lots of them. Several skiers can keep a trail packed and tracked. Sometimes a poling-lane also needs to be skied in if the side parts of a trail get too deep and soft.

A pulk-sled can be built with old skis screwed to the bottom at the correct width then pulled to set a ski-track. Using rigid towing poles crossed over lets

Pic above from "Whack Jobs," a film about bike grooming in Michigan! Snowbikers love the flowy handling of singletrack. ...I know skiers who dig it, too.

the sled track nicely behind a skier. Load the sled with some weight – like a kid! (I've made bungie-poles with electrical conduit, dowels and bungie cord to let me smoothly stride ahead of a pulk with two kids aboard. They smoothly glide along without getting their heads jerked around. The pulk doesn't start and stop with the pulses of skiing. The poles expand a couple feet with each stride, evening out the efforts.)

When snow is too deep, one really should, just head over to your gladed slopes. It's time for turns! Today's BC and tele skis perform so well and are so wide that you don't actually need much powder for a powder day.

Skiing Singletrack Groomed for Bikes

Ski resorts and multi-use areas today often offer trails groomed and designed for fat-bikes to enjoy the snow. These offer an untracked, narrow, square tread and go for flow to accommodate the speed and handling of snowbiking. But other users, like snowshoers and snow-runners -- and skiers! -- can use these trails, too. They can be some of the funnest trails around! ...Even without any ski-track grooves.

Now, skis don't have brakes and these trails are narrow so a few tricks will help you safely enjoy them. Shorter midlength skis are smart, as are wider skis with metal edges and BC bindings to add braking power even to small moves. Dragging a ski in the deep snow outside the track will slow you some. Both skis will slow you more. Dragging poles helps.

Ideally, skiers would be involved in the grooming set-up and help fund and encourage a somewhat wider-set track if that's helpful. An 18" trail might work fine for fatbikes but it isn't really skiable. 25" is the minimum for including room to pole and 30" is better. Money talks, as does work. Bikers might be talked into a trail that's wide enough for poling and snow-plowing -- if the skiers pitch in.

Nowadays all snow trail users are reminded of sustainability values. Skiers have long known to not skate over classic set tracks. And hikers have long been encouraged to not walk on ski tracks. But snowbikers are leading the way in crafting policy for mutual non-interfering use. Follow their lead and join in.

A big risk for trail damage is when tires press a "U" groove into the trail which then sets up overnight. This snaking channel -- even if it's 10" wide -- then disturbs all subsequent trail users, including bikers, until it's re-groomed.

Worst is when any kind of users heavily mark up a melted trail which refreezes over night.

Thoughtful use lets a trail serve the most users for the longest time before needing new snow or regrooming.

Snowbike groomers come in many flavors, from machines to models you pull on snowshoes or with a bike.

A weighted ice-fishing sled pulled by a fatbike with pulk-rods is a thrifty option for modest trail packing.

The My Trail Groomer company offers affordable models for $150-250. They offer bike, classic-ski, and skate-skiing groomers in various widths.

The simplest bike grooming method of all is when riders do laps a few inches left and right wide of center and intentionally pack a wide, flat tread with their tires. Efforts toward at least an 18" tread pay off with a trail that works better for everyone.

Seasonal Ebb & Flow

Snow can be a rabbit-hole of awesome. Different kinds of skiing and snowfun fit with all the kinds of snow. With plenty of overlap. Every season offers us some of each, more or less. As climate change reduces the overall amount of snow many of us get all it really does is mess with the ratios and quantities, but every year still sees some of each. It's like the correct answer to the question "How many skis/bikes do you own?" … Answer: "One of each!" Weather is the same way! Along with how we respond to it. (Also, again, the best defense against climate disaster is awareness: get outside now, in the winter, which will change the most. Then be willing to change everything to save the world. It won't really be that big of a pain. It'll bring people together. It'll only change the fortunes of a few billionaires and they'll likely adapt just fine to new investment opportunities.)

The establishment view of skiing only promotes a winter style that runs from "medium snow" to "hardpacked."

But SPRING is a ski season! There is so much more to skiing than we're told or sold.

First, there are two ski seasons: winter plus an equally wonderful SPRING happening AFTER the days start getting longer and AFTER the sun starts coming out more and the snow starts changing.

Each phase of the ski season has kinds of snowfun that suit it to a tee.

Learn your local snow holding lore. Different trails and skiable areas will offer the best experiences at different times of year and in different conditions of snow.

A winter season might have a flow something like this: *early false starts of snowfall on unfrozen ground, *frozen ground with light snowcover, *light snow cover that gets a bit more on top and STARTS OUR SKIING ENGINES!, *medium snows, *heavy snows, *really cold days, *hardpacked snow, *old snow, *icy rock-hard snow, *partial melts, *warm days, *total melt offs, *dry cold days, *warm days and cold nights then cold days that create CRUST for free skiing everywhere all day, *total melt-offs followed by a few days of a cold snap to give clear black strong flexible 2-3" ice for skating, *warming days that weaken the crust and shorten the windows for crust-skiing, *crust skiing only

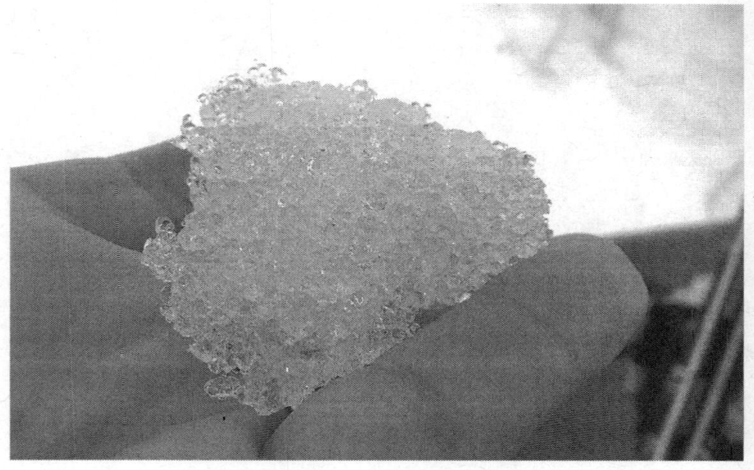

Corn snow -- juicy, sparkly, strong, fast, soft. The stuff of the second awesome ski season: springtime!

Wide grooming makes for perfect skate-skiing. Surface holds up to large numbers of skiers. But the striding track at the side often has to take a non-ideal line around downhill curves where good tracks would be very helpful. ...Downsides of road-width grooming are less character, fewer features, big machine expense and carbon footprint.

on the north sides of shady woodlots and windrows, *warm days followed by cold nights and ever-warming sunnier days that transform the powder snow or crust into loose granular snow, *more such days that turn the granular snow into full-on corn snow, *enduring days of corn, *mid-morning to early-afternoon periods of corn, *good corn only in shady forests or on the north sides of shady lots and windrows, *pleasant hiking between smaller patches of wonderful corn snow, *much water in the snow, rivulets and slush with corn snow, corn snow amid more hiking, mud and flowing melt-off creeks.

Crust & Corn: 2 Kinds of Heaven

I have to doubly or triply emphasize spring skiing. Ski season isn't just winter. And winter proper isn't always cold. Spring skiing is a favorite for many. Those who aren't savvy can overlook it. As soon as the snow starts melting maybe they switch right over to biking. Well, sure, start biking! ...But don't put away your skis just yet!

You were happy in winter. It was fun being warm when it was cold. But now is another big pay-off. Spring is easy on the body. Easy for picnics. No need to bundle up. It's a time for t-shirt skiing Get a face tan. Sun warms the forest floor dry in places. Skunk cabbage and jack-in-the-pulpit come out.

The air is full of clean humid negative ions and the smells of earth. Sometimes you have to walk between snowfields. Resorts eventually stop grooming and close. It's yet another chance to earn your turns. It's so comfy for picnics. Birds are singing and animals are coming back out. You'll see more critter tracks.

We will still get fresh snowfalls. Don't moan! Change your gears from winter to spring skiing!

...And now you can have the best corn and crust skiing imaginable!

If the snow is still holding in shady forests, you'll likely want to still do classic stride skiing on the singletrack. But you can also find shaded aspects of open terrain next to northern treelines or hedgerows. These open places might be windswept and drift-prone early in the season. But now, after a few cycles of freeze/thaw in the cooler early mornings, these areas can offer wonderful **crust** skiing, where the snow will support the weight of a skier, letting you ski anywhere -- and enjoy some wide-open skate-skiing.

It takes experimentation and exploration to find what works! You'll become a connoisseur of this new more weather-variegated kind of winter world. Indeed, crust sometimes happens best in semi-shaded areas, with shadier places staying powdery even as it warms and sunny places losing all their snow.

Thanks to climate change, crust can also come on during the cold mid-winter when we get surprise thaws amid typically low temps. If you can stand on the snow anywhere you can ski on it everywhere!

This brings us to a heaven-sent aspect of spring skiing: ***corn snow***. After snow freezes and thaws a few times, it turns into robust, juicy, large granules called corn. This can be enjoyably skied in many ways (klister!) at various times of day until it's too warm to be stable, then you have to let it rest again in hopes of a cooler night which will deliver bliss to you again the next morning. ...Not too early when it's too firm, the dreaded 'boilerplate.' You have to catch it at just the right time.

Once you experience the joy of the transitional spring time of year (as well as other thaw cycles) you'll learn that at this time of year you need to re-arrange your work schedule for special morning duties offsite for an hour or so -- corn time is often best between 9am and noon.

Spring skiing is a wonderfully bittersweet time. Over the course of weeks or a month you'll be saying a slow goodbye to skiing for awhile. Grand finale ski deck parties start popping up. We usually keep skiing until we can't. We're willing to walk quite a ways between our cherished last snow patches. (It's great that today's skis are so easy to take on and off.)

Using Up the Snow

Traffic levels on the trails are relevant. Casual ungroomed trails can offer perfect conditions – until they get overly skied-in, or walked-on, or U-channeled by snowbikers. You can keep alternative possibilities for trails in the background for when they are needed.

Remember: unlike all the work that has to go into making terrain suitable for biking, skiing can be done anywhere there is snow. And it can easily be done to leave no trace.

So, if one trail gets too icy from too much use, you might be able to just track in another trail a few feet off to the side of it, or use entirely different routes through the same given woodlot to get fresh snow.

You can probably guess that glade-skiing BC hounds guard their terrain as assiduously as surfboard gangs control access to their favorite breaking waves. How much traffic can a snowy glade bear? Answer: only as much as someone tossed aside deadfall from fall-lines the previous autumn.

Also, you efficiently ski up all the available acreage of snow by moving each run over a mere foot or two to get at fresh snow. Then follow the sun around your secret bowl.

Grooming

When we go to a groomed ski area, what kind of XC opportunities do we find? First, there might be a fee. Which will be microscopic compared to alpine skiing, even if snowmaking is involved. Most ski trails today are groomed in the double-track style or wider. Groomer machines pack in and carve out two sets of classic tracks so skiers can ski side by side and also easily pass. Then alongside that 6-foot width of trail might be another 8 feet of smoothly packed corduroy designed for skate-skiing. Thus the common ski resort Nordic setup is a 14-ft wide lane between the trees or through the fields or golf course. (That's for us mortals. Elite courses, especially for sprints, need room for several skiers to be able to pass at the same time and so can be 30 feet wide!) The topography has to be modified with bulldozers in the off-season so that the ski-groomer can manage the uphills, drops and corners. It's a bit like grading a single-lane road. Such grooming lets what snowfalls last a long time and serve many skiers before wearing out into hard grey ice. The groomers are usually equipped with devices that re-process hardpacked icy snow into a manageable surface. Such machines can easily cost $100k. These machines are cool, but their significant overheads also include carbon emissions. (Snowmobile trail systems are much more extensive and use this same equipment, though mostly of the bigger type.)

Classic tracks can be afterthoughts on courses with a skating emphasis. Tracks merely set to one side of a trail can be impossible to use when turns aren't conducive. The skis just won't stay in them, especially on fast downhills where they're critical. You can also get the hint that striding is less a priority when you keep getting whipped by branches when you're skiing the tracks on the side -- even though striding is naturally the biggest ski demographic, or potentially so. Of course, trails that are tracked in ways that discourage striding -- or even crash-out or lash striders -- will see the self-fulfilling prophecy of "we don't get many striders here" -- which may well also correlate to a trail that doesn't earn as much profit for the area as it could even if it serves "a lot" of skaters.

Occasionally a trail system will also offer a singletrack classic trail, or a double-tracked trail without a skating lane. This lets a trail be narrower and the machine needed to set just one track can be a simple snowmobile and such a trail can be designed anywhere a snowmobile can go.

Many resorts are proud of a daily grooming schedule where all trails are freshened up at night then allowed to set up before the next day's skiers arrive.

At alpine areas, grooming is also a point of pride. Fresh corduroy is the ticket for both Nordic and Alpine skiing. But elite alpine free-skiing happens beyond grooming. Skiing "groomer" runs is typically a blue-level skill: smooth, fast, and easy. With Nordic skiing, the love of grooming runs all the way to the top. Skiers and staff alike are extremely aware of the art and the reward of good grooming. The many kinds of snow conditions each require their own special processing for best results.

Some XC resorts also offer groomed snowshoe and snowbike trails.

There isn't yet a parallel for more challenge in XC to the terrain parks enjoyed at nearly all alpine resorts.

The Thrill of Skiing Groomers

Groomed trails are awesome to ski. They run the whole range of skill levels and are signed accordingly. They can be designed for classic skiing, skate-skiing or both. They're a magic carpet ride for skiers. They're a smooth ribbon flowing out into a forest, offering the fastest glide and the most predictable grip. You can use the slenderest of skis and still have wonderful stability. The grooves let classic skiers hold a relaxed tuck downhill through thrillingly fast bends. It's like a slot car! A groomed trail gives the ultimate work-surface for skiing.

All official XC today is groomed. Groomed trails don't just happen. They are designed. At the better ski resorts a huge amount of thought goes into laying out a groomed trail so that it delivers a peak experience for all skiers. It's a year-round effort to create and care for a proper ski trail. They're built in summer, rocks removed, graded, seeded, mowed. In winter, covered with packed, cared-for snow, they work with your momentum, undulating, ebbing and flowing, working their way to crescendoes.

They'll be designed with safe bends, corners, and run-outs. You can let your skis run and safely glide as fast as you can imagine. 40mph is possible on some trails. Some challenging downhills are even designed with prejumps like an alpine downhill race course, where the slope has rises and drops within an overall descent. A skier has to be on the top of their game to enjoy such a trail! Absorb the rise then fall away with the change in pitch. But what a thrill!

A groomed ski trail can be enjoyed with the thinnest, lightest and fastest of skis while still giving sufficient stability and control.

Grooming lets a given snowfall support

Eli gets it on. With abandon. All in! ...On his way to a top race finish.

(photo courtesy Tim Potter)

more skiers at a high quality of skiing. Ungroomed trails tend to wash out and get icy especially in the corners after a week or so of use by dozens of skiers. If a couple hundred people flock to a trail they can "ski it up" in a day without grooming.

Liability concerns and wide grooming resulted in today's more moderate trails.

However, every other outdoor sport in the meantime has ratcheted up the thrills aspect and skills on advanced terrain. Maybe XC skiing will regain a reputation for challenge.

Beginner and intermediate trails are designed just as carefully as the advanced: to deliver just the right blend of challenge and reward in the available terrain.

Trails usually are designed with a direction in mind, though some sections might be two-way.

I note that many ski trails were designed in the 60's and 70's, updated a bit in the 80's for skating and liability, and not touched since. I find that some are not designed to modern flow specs and often include a few ridiculously sharp turns at the bottom of fast hills that take the fun out. Maybe they were designed in the days of slower skis.

Trail Ratings

The universal trail difficulty rating system is used at official XC and MTB trail systems and is explained on many maps and trailhead signs but it's worth repeating. The system uses words, shape, color and marking. It's hard to find a great summary, but this should help. Note, ratings are based on good conditions.

Beginner = green circle with slightly wavy mark = gentle terrain that gives you chances to use basic skills. Often shorter.

Intermediate = blue triangle with "S" mark = terrain has faster hills, tighter turns, longer climbs, requiring all skills, some to be combined or used one after the other while in gliding transitions -- good fitness is helpful.

Expert = black square with zig-zag mark = terrain is steep and big with fast turns, requiring all skills to be used together or in quick succession, repeatedly -- broad-scope fitness is required (quickness, power and endurance).

Caution = yellow triangle with red exclamation mark = pay attention now! Often used to highlight a challenging downhill.

Double black diamond = rare in XC, but could be narrower and rougher with downhills that change pitch and direction beyond the line of sight or include rises in downhills that could send you airborne without a pre-jump. Expertise is required for safety but trail has risks even at that.

The Thrill of Racing

How is racing different from regular skiing? How is ski-racing different from other kinds of racing? There are a lot of commonalities. Let's see if I can find some distinctions.

Well, there's spectating and fandom. It's thrilling to watch the top-shelf action: the World Cup, Olympics, big Loppets, and the Birkie! These are courses and athlete beyond normal comprehension. They're inspiring and awing.

Pondering racing can be a critique as much as a promotion. And I'll try not to make claims for the bestness of skiing compared to other sport. Instead I'll try to describe specific distinctions. Yet I can't avoid making some generalizations that aren't always publicized.

Yes, I'm ambivalent about racing. I'm highly susceptible to the fever, but can consider the bigger picture. I've seen what competition can do to community for better and worse. There are pro's, con's, risks, costs. Races can be fun, but there's more going on.

One of the uniquenesses of racing is the quiet. You might be among hundreds of other skiers and … it'll be quiet. Race pace is faster than chat pace. And it might strike you as eerie if you haven't experienced it before. But this isn't unique to skiing per se.

Another odd thing is that after the first few minutes of a race the finishing order will be established very close to what it will look like at the end. This makes a race a lot like a poker hand. Preparation the main thing. Your potential will be apparent soon after the start, if not well before it. But, again, this isn't unique to skiing.

All this can make a wizened vet like me wonder: why don't we make it a 1km race then go out for a big fun group ski? Or, if everyone went only 10% slower we could all be chatting and having fun and getting to know each other. Why can't we have our cake and eat it, too?

Racing isn't literally important, it's a fabricated challenge, one that we create. This gives us a key: racing is story-telling.

We hope for good stories. The organizer sets the stage. The racers are the actors. And every race has a winner. They are the fastest, sure, but they also have a role to play. They represent their community, where they come from, and once they win, they represent the race. Sportsmanship is a drama. And all of us in a race are role models. Sure, we also are every other day, but during the race, the spotlight is on us.

Back to the "idraet" of the Norwegians that I mentioned in the Intro: it took awhile to convince them to let their unique winter sport into the competitive arena. They were concerned their story of sportsmanship might not shine clear through any venal striving to one-up someone else.

The downsides are worth mentioning: obsession, addiction, injury, sickness, expense, myopia, fragmentation, segregation. If we can be moderate, let's proceed…

Here are a few of the 8,000 skiers racing the Birkie. The elite waves go all-out for over two hours.

Notice the classic strider on the left. He's a front-runner in his category and is doing pretty well mixed in with the skaters.

The majority of skiers are skiing with their friends and just seeing how it goes, enjoying the beautiful course, trying to finish in good spirits or to improve on last year, as in any marathon.

Casual community-level racing.

Once you enter, get ready! Everyone will be there, game on. Maybe you've been skiing by yourself or with a few friends. How might you fare against the world?

But let's not downplay racing yourself. ...Or, I suppose, racing each other online via Strava. Whenever we go out and hammer a trail as fast as we can we're racing! Especially when we give it our all. A big part of racing, though, is competing. It's also worth noting that if we make ourselves our rival we can get more carried away than when others are!

Early in race history, excelling at one kind of skiing was nothing to be proud of. A proper ski event included all aspects of skiing. The winning Ski Meister was usually the one who did the best overall after races in Slalom, Cross Country and Jumping. Even today there are still multi-disciplinary Ski Meister titles. Also, a single course could test the full range of skills.

A race can be a goal for your ski learning process. You can aim for a race after a couple months of skiing to see what's what. Or you can use a race as a loppet or an opportunity to ski on a special day with a bunch of other people on a trail system set aside just for you that day. The groomers and host are pulling out all the stops to help you have a wonderful time. Or it can be all of this and more!

Skiing any day can be a chance to give "all you got," a race is just more-so. It's often not even safe to go all-out on a trail during a normal day. Other people might be on the trail doing their own thing so you need to be careful. On race day the course is yours. One of its distinctions is that skiers can experience going a lot harder than other forms of racing, maybe even surprising themselves with how much they can tolerate.

Race organizers often go all-out to deliver a real challenge. So if you think you've experienced big uphills and downhills before, doing a race gives you a chance to perhaps greatly increase your previous downhill speed record, or awe you with how big of an uphill you're facing.

A big aspect of ski racing compared to a typical outing is huge, fast downhills where you can find yourself crowded in with many other skiers! Everyone has to keep their nerve! Crashes can happen all around you -- hopefully you can dodge them all!

Organizers might offer a range of distances and challenges. It used to be in the US that ski-racing was more like a running race, where most of the participants were casually in search of simply having more fun than usual with their friends. As I've mentioned, skiing in many places has since the 1970's become more serious and the fields smaller. Still, tours are often offered on race days. "Loppet" is a term often used to describe a tour, but it can also be a race. Usually a loppet will at least have a tour option.

In the US we have junior racing, high-school, local races, regional races, national series, small USCSA colleges (formerly NCSA), NCAA, factory teams and national teams. In the Olympics, XC skiing is part of Cross Country Skiing, Combined Skiing (with Ski Jumping), and Biathlon.

A global series of popular long-distance Worldloppets has for decades been offered as part of a tourism bucket-list. Long ago, a Worldloppet Passport was developed. Just doing one of these events is a big feat, but some travel the world checking them off over the years.

There are 20 premier Worldloppets around the world. Several of the biggest attract up to 15,000 skiers. They are often part of weeklong snowsport celebrations.

They have elite racers as a tiny upper fraction of participants. These are typically non-Olympians yet top-ranked regional athletes. These are the legacy races, some almost 100 years old. At 40-90km, they are sometimes longer than marathons. They also usually feature terrain that is either gentle or larger in scope, with miles of gradual uphills and long descents. Courses are wide, designed to support heavy traffic.

In the US, we have the North American Birkebeiner in Wisconsin, featuring big roller-type hills and 10,000 racers for a weekend of events, with 20,000 fans and family. Canada has the Gatineau Loppet.

XC racing is big in Europe and even bigger in Scandinavia. We should remember the 1994 Winter Olympics in Lillehammer Norway where there were something like 100,000 spectators out on the course, in the forests, for days, camping in little tent and bonfire villages of fandom, watching their heroes, and cheering them so loudly that basically none of the racers could hear or think. In Vordenberg's memoir of that experience he said he forgot to factor in not being able to sense his own heartbeat due to the noise of the crowds all along the course. (Too bad an Italian won the relay sprint.)

Here are two other distinctive long-standing events, giving a further view of the variety in XC:

The Grand Traverse from Crested Butte to Aspen in Colorado is a race in the new/old Ski-Mo tradition (ski mountaineering). It's a 40-mile race over 7000 feet of mountain passes at night (to reduce avalanche risk) unmarked and with a few

Skiers were just as fierce, and the action as intense, back in the day.

big features, each many miles long: a lot of up then a lot of down, with river crossings. It's done with a partner and safety gear. Winning teams now use Alpine Touring gear. Occasional crazies still try skate-skiing.

The Canadian Ski Marathon isn't a race. It's the world's longest ski marathon and thousands have done it over the past 50 years. The highlight of a variety of events on CSM weekend is a 99-mile route between Montreal and Ottawa. It's a community-run event featuring three levels of accomplishment, required to be achieved in order: Bronze, Silver and Gold Coureur des Bois. Your first year's level is to

ski the route. Next you can ski it wearing at least a 5kg pack and you sleep wherever you like. Lastly, you get Gold if you ski the route, carry your gear and use it to camp outside next to a bonfire with your very own bale of straw, provided.

How Does Racing Feel?

How is a ski race different from any other, like a running or bike race? The uniqueness of skiing, and ski-racing, is the smooth white sheet that is your playing field. It is quite pure. There will typically be plenty of room for you to lay it all out there. And because skiing is an all-body activity, the snow is happy to receive your personal maximum of VO2-Max, power, fitness, aerobics...and skill.

Because it uses arms and legs and core and is weight-bearing, XC skiing uses more of your whole body's ability to put out energy than other sports. (This doesn't mean it's tougher in any other sense.) Its highly conducive platform -- packed snow -- is part of why we can go so hard at it. It's a sport where "seeing stars" is a common occurrence throughout even one event. "Going under" is easy to do most any-time during a race. In a running race, for instance, people usually can't easily doing something that makes it likely they'll pass out at a lot of points during the race. Since you use your whole body, with skiing if you're not careful you can easily go too hard. The good thing is that it's not likely you'll get hurt. Snow is not like pavement, or swimming in open water. Snow is often quite cushy. Sure, be careful, keep your wits about you as best you can, but a wide snow-trail is a good place to learn about getting cross-eyed and going harder-than-hard.

Anyone doing XC skiing will get fit. With racing you'll get fitter. But every sport has its tendencies. Skiing is not really about tactics, teamwork, explosiveness or agility. At its pinnacle it's about lean muscle spread over the whole body generating the most overall watts output humanly possible while maintaining good technique.

For most citizen-level classic racing, double-poling is the main thing since most modern race courses are rather mellow, so it rewards a canoe-racer's upper body plus the aerobics of a runner. And, frankly, it's boring, pneumatic, less-skilled and has hurt the sport. If trail skiing ever became a thing then more leg, striding, dynamism, and skill would re-enter the classic picture. At the World Cup level, legs indeed are in the picture due to the hilliness of their courses, designed in reaction against doublepoling. Subtle skill is also desirable since classic is considered the subtler discipline that takes longer to learn.

For skate-ski racing, all-around VO2-Max with gifts both above and below the waist are needed. Its reputation for straight-forward technique probably more readily holds true at the citizen level. Still, I have to think there's a lot of potential for subtle skill. After all, it's well-known that both paddlesport and ice speed-skating are extremely technical. Skate-skiing combines upper and lower and certainly brings many technical issues into play. Just finding out how your unique body and style is best expressed is a long-term, ongoing challenge ... and possible point of endur-ing fascination.

Upper body aerobic power has taken on new relevance at the upper levels of all of today's groomed-course type racing, moving from super-fit into the monster level. (It can't hurt to be able to knock out about 50 pull-ups, pushups, and dips in like 3 minutes.) It's not so much that poling has become more important, just there was more room for improved upper body fitness.

People who like to race who have a lot of leg tend to gravitate to running or biking. Those with upper body wattage go for swimming and canoe racing. Maybe rock-climbing. If you enjoy energy output with both arms and legs and you're not over 6'5" (where rowing might lure you away) then XC might be conducive to big thrills and top results.

Race Culture

The night before a race is frequently a special time for racer friends to get together for waxing. They'll have beers and a boombox playing. At a big event there might be a big area set aside for waxing and you'll be with many strangers, making new friends. Some might be secretive about their concoctions. Some will be desperately asking for advice. If word spreads about a fast wax there might be begging and bargaining.

Nowadays with the internet the main wax companies will also be testing or what's working that weekend in that region or for that specific race, and will post what they've found works best. They like to show how to best use their products.

When it's cold but the snow is too thin to ski, Nordic ice-skating lets us explore interesting waterways and enjoy great glide. These free-heel skates are easy on/off, letting us use ski boots and bindings. They are tolerant of lumpy ice, snow and poor technique.

They share secrets freely. ...But even they might keep their very best tips in reserve for their stars. Then, too, some skiers and wax technicians know that combinations of products from different companies are the best. This will be harder beta intel to get.

A race is also a chance for strategy, for jockeying for position. You'll ideally want to have a start that ends with you being where you want to be during the race. In ski racing as in bike racing or running you can both draft off of others or pace off of them. You'll likely be with a group that is skiing similar to you. Maybe you can tuck in with them. Maybe hanging with them is taking all you have. You might find places where you're faster than they are or where you need to be careful not to be dropped. You'll probably keep trying to move up to whatever placing in the race is letting you give it your all.

A strange feeling can happen if you find yourself at the front: suddenly there's nobody to pace off of! You're the rabbit for everyone else!

Skiing is somewhat unusual in that if you move up in the ranks and start doing more serious events you might find yourself doing individual-start races in addition to mass-start. It's also a way for a big group to race on a narrow trail. Individual-start is like a time trial in biking: skiers are sent off alone or with another skier at intervals. Once you get into the higher ranks you can appreciate it since the result can be said to be more pure.

Some famous races, like the Birkie, make you start near the back your first year no matter how many races you've won beforehand. Working your way up in the Birkie takes years.

Some people catch the racing bug bigtime. Personally, I hope they look before they leap. Normal skiing (and normal life) can include such a nice variety while racing can become specialized and all-consuming. Another aspect of racing nowadays is becoming a fan of regional, national and global racing on TV and the internet. The biggest online race streams and videos might not be in English but enthusiasts find heroes to root for, and occasionally villains to boo.

Then there's the idea that a race is a consumer product being marketed to us. We pay and the staff serves us. Maybe the race is a fundraiser and a whole town or community volunteers to make it happen. Yes, a race is about participation but it's also part of consumerism. Be a good customer! More buy-in helps us avoid pitfalls: join a club and help host your own annual race.

Volunteer so you can appreciate the other side of the race-bib.

A quirky thing about racing which is obvious but sometimes easy to overlook is that even though a race day is especially set aside, anything can happen. I suggestion doing your best to keep perspective. Still, a big goal brings high hopes and expectations creep in. ...Along with maybe a bad head cold that hits on race morning. In these days of climate change, the weather and snow could be in any condition when the race starts or change wildly during it. The main thing is that everyone is in the same boat. A sudden cold front. A blizzard! A rainstorm! The groomer makes a mistake and accidentally churns up a layer of ice cubes which becomes your new race course -- oops! Or grooms too late the night before and the weather changes and the snow doesn't set up and it's all soft as mashed potatoes! Or hard as a rock! Everybody has to do their best with what happens. (Some people -- like me! -- like it when crazy conditions come along, considering adversity more their friend than others. "NOW we have a race!" Adaptability and pain-tolerance are harder to shop for.)

But this isn't different from any other sport. It's just something that people might not notice when they're first starting. Also, as Greg said, it doesn't get easier, you just go faster. And faster isn't all that different.

You get fit, but also have stress, bills, boredom, injury, sickness that you wouldn't have otherwise. The downsides are real. Evaluate them in light of your goals.

There is a range of events to choose from to suit your druthers, from sprints to marathons.

Ski-racing doesn't really offer a beginner rank, but you can take this as a compliment: you can line up near the best. Bigger events often have wave starts, some being self-seeded based on your expected finishing time. Sometimes a "fun event" will be offered in addition to a "real" race. A nuance is that for many races there will be a category that's part of a points series. So you can pick the other one if you want to ski with people of less intensity. Like, a classic race might be for points that weekend, but a skating category might be also offered: the less-serious racers will do that. Or if the big event is a marathon, then a half-marathon might be offered for those who are less gung-ho.

Course profiles can do quite a bit to select for success. Many races today are laid out on a gentle route and are biased

Snowshoeing is awesome whenever the snow is too deep and soft for skiing. Miracle float is wonderful to experience. Modern shoes often sink more than is enjoyable. I'd think a 160 lb person could get tolerable float with XL moderns. With their crampon-like bindings they seem best for icy or sidehill conditions. I rarely use moderns.

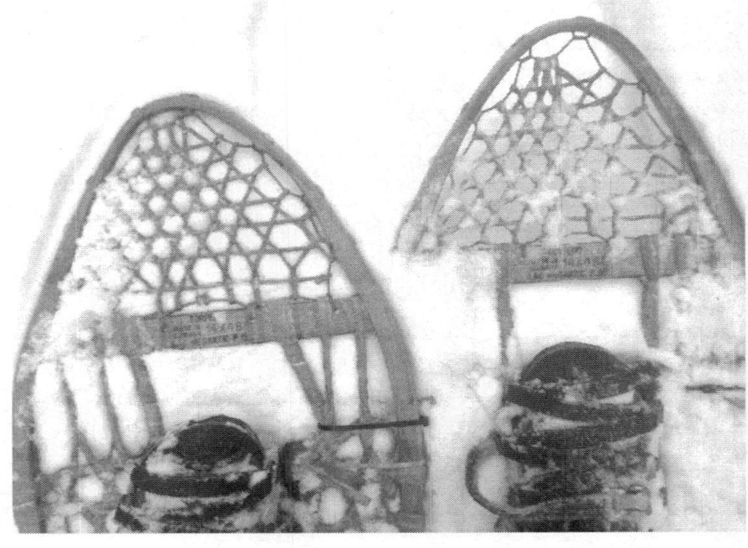

to powerful physiques. If you have a big upper body you might be in luck, especially in a classic race, where everyone might doublepole the whole time. However, if you happen to encounter a really hilly course then skinnier, lighter, more leg-oriented skiers might tend to place higher.

Racing is cool and all, but the Women's Ski Tour brings thousands of women together and into winter fun thanks to a carefree "ski party" attitude.

Dopage

Doping is a reality today at all levels for those looking for top results -- perhaps more so among XC skiers than other sports. Doping is creeping into the amateur ranks in many sports. Why would XC be immune?

A recent buzzword to consider is the "TUE"--therapeutic use exemption. This is legal doping under doctor's orders. Over half the medalists in XC at a recent Olympics suffered from asthma, a usually debilitating disorder.

Doping is an indicator of a larger desperate, opportunist mindset that affects all sport as people push for any edge. Even clean athletes can have kitchens that look like pharmacies, full of OTC supplements.

One way to approach the issue might be to always consider oneself an underdog, since you can't ever know what your rivals are doing. All the more reason to remember the relativity of sport.

Doesn't spending a lot of money on gear, wax and tech services also buy advantage? Yet this "arms race" is accepted. The net of racing hauls in many things, including rationalizations. Play at your risk!

Nordic *ICE* Skating

Many years here in mid-Michigan we'll get a total melt-off in mid-January followed by a hard freeze even the next day. Then a week of dry cold conditions. There's no snow for skiing, but… This is when we get our sweet black lake ice. It's perfectly smooth and clear. You can even see fish and turtles swimming around down below. As long as you have 2-3" and the ice is fresh, strong and elastic we often have a good week of speed skating we enjoy. In such conditions I'll use Nordic Skates instead of traditional speedskates. They are so easy to use. They work great. And they are extremely forgiving of wild ice with its occasional defects, rough spots, slush or crusty snow. No more trip-up's when the heel is free. I'll bring ski-poles if it's thinnish. Then I'll also wear a PFD – helps keep me warm as well! The ski poles would also be useful for a self-rescue. I keep the carbide tips sharp both for poling performance on ice and for secure emergency grip. I'll also carry a rope, towel, spare shirt, socks and pants in a rucksack. No sense being uncomfortable for long if I take a soaker. I've been doing this for decades and haven't had a problem yet. Ya know, the water is maybe 40 degrees -- warmer than the air. I've gone swimming, in winter, twice in my life in surprise situations, and broke through ice once -- it wasn't such a big deal. I also tell my wife where I'm going and when I'll be home. And bring a phone. Really, use the buddy system whenever skating on wild ice: take a friend along. (Of course that's best for safety and fun anywhere!)

What I've noticed during marginal weather times like this is that inexperienced ice adventurers don't realize that ice near the shore is thinnest. Also that ice near or over organic matter is thinner. A wide path from shore to thick ice can freeze strong, but I've often seen casual hikers stroll off through heavy cattails on their way to or from ice. This is where they could easily fall through. The water might not be deep but if it's cold hypothermia is an issue. Also, deep mud below the water could be a big problem, bogging down a struggling person.

Snowshoeing -- When it's Deep!

If you also have some favorite dense terrain and the snow keeps coming, once it's over a foot on the ground don't forget to put your snowshoes to good use. It's what they're made for! When the trailpack isn't firm enough for any sort of kick'n'glide, it's time for pure flotation. Snowshoes are awesome as a way to easily get around when nothing else works. They're magic angel wings. I find that 14"x48" Michigan-shape wooden shoes are best for me at 180lbs. They're wide, yet they have tails for tracking and upturned toes for easy forward swing. They float better than any modern shoes in the conditions that snowshoes are suited for. I find that modern shoes work great merely for improving traction on packed trails that otherwise would almost be fine for walking in snowboots. Or, moderns are good for a packed tread that doesn't quite have enough strength to support bare boots. Any snowshoe is better than post-holing! Moderns

Sniff… looks like the season is over. Time to put away the quiver, etc., into its various cubbyholes in the garage.

Skiing and dogs go great together. ...In the backcountry. Ski-joring opens a new world of fun and thrills with your furry friends. So many of them love to please, learn, run and pull!

are also awesome for sideslopes, ice, and dense brush. But when pure float is what you want, big woodies deliver like nothing else!

Skijoring!

And what about skijoring!? That's the sport of skiing with your dog pulling you. Dogs love skiing! They can just pull you along if you like, or you can ski while they are pulling and you both can then just go along more easily.

Dogs aren't allowed at any downhill resorts and so our mainstream winter culture isn't used to considering dogs as key players. Nordic centers will have often a trail where dogs are allowed because they know how much people love skiing with dogs, but doublecheck this for any groomed ski trails. (And for sure always pick up after your pooch!) Everywhere else that's snowy they love to romp.

Dogs can learn the simple commands needed to do beautiful teamwork with on trails as easily as they can learn to please you doing anything else. They love to learn and are always proud to show you what they know and what they can do. They can help you go faster, farther. Dogs and skis go together! ...More than one dog works,

too!

So, get a dog and harness, train it to pull, and give a huge boost to your winter fun. Include your dog in your ski day! ("Skijor With Your Dog" by Mari Hoe-Raitto is an awesome book.)

It's a whole extra dimension for skiing that is 100% reasonably doable and hugely enjoyable.

Most casual singletrack is fair game for winter fun with dogs. Just "do no harm" to a trail. Even with a casual mixed-use trail, if the local scene hasn't included dogs and if other users delight in keeping their skied-in track looking and working good, don't hurt it. Keep the dog off to the side. If you classic ski behind your dog you're usually automatically patching your divots.

A dog can really help pulling gear for camping. ...AND keep you warm at night!

Our daily range can be curtailed when pulling a pulk. Put your dog on the front and go farther while taking it easier when hauling gear!

I've seen rigs where a compact gear sled is rigged between dog and skier. It's not a dog-sled, but designed for ski-joring.

A Wealth of Variety

In low snow country we don't get tons of powder or long-lasting, reliable cold packed conditions. But in terms of variety we can step out ahead. Now, this variety can come and go quickly, so be ready to grab it! It also has darn low overhead, so it ain't no big thing to change it up. With a few simple pieces of gear we can enjoy a dozen different ways to ski.

Culture: Our XC Situation

Great News for USA Ski Racing!

US ski racing has finally made it! I'm so happy that I had to rewrite this section! On February 21, 2018, Jessie Diggins and Kikkan Randall won the first-ever Olympic gold in XC for the USA. And with such passion! US skiing will never be the same. Their win in the Team Sprint in Korea is a game-changer for the US. It shows a lot of things, not least of which is the "all in" team spirit and social good cheer that the US Women's Team brings -- especially Jessie (even though she wouldn't want to be singled out). Winter and skiing are about friendly fun, people!

There'd been a drought on any US Olympic XC medals since 1976 when Bill Koch won silver all by himself. The let-down at our poor results in the next Games in 1980 played a big part in the subsequent collapse of a hugely booming XC scene in the US.

It's finally a new era!

The US presence on the world stage has recently been gradually improving, achieving its highest levels of success thanks especially to the women's team, explicitly cheerleaded by super-fun Jessie. Several women have been winning or finishing on the podium of the biggest races.

This new era could readily be leveraged, except that XC has lost a lot of its brick'n'mortar retail base and instructor resources except in a few hotspots.

There was an XC Boom? The Heck?

Millions of folks in the USA used to know about Nordic skiing. It's hard to imagine, but 500,000 pairs of XC skis were sold here in 1979! Interest had built through the 60's and 70's as America became interested in the environment and the outdoors ... and reality.

It's amazing how popular outdoor sports were back then even though products were low tech and hard to use compared to today.

But since the 1980's most outdoor shops have closed, especially XC ski shops and departments. By 1981 XC had dropped an astounding ten-fold to 50k! Probably no sport has dropped so fast. We've since recovered to 100k skis sold annually, but sales are focused on our few hot-spots.

Finding the good snow can involve trial-and-error. If it's not skiable in one place, think about it: you might know another place nearby that holds snow better. We did.

Thin, translucent snow is a type we now see more often. We've grown fond of it, its juiciness, and the leaves we see floating in and under it. It is great for skiing.

Regions where reliable snow has declined have really lost out.

What happened? The early 70's climb of US XC ski sales was noticed by Norway. An overseas consortium hugely stepped up production before the 1980 Lake Placid Olympics. There was giddiness at the prospect of Bill Koch performing even better than his previous silver medal in 1976. Gold was in sight in more ways than one! But winter decided to make a late appearance, and Koch didn't respond well to the pressure of the limelight. And the imports included a lot of junk. The US market tanked. Which caused a disastrous glut in Europe. Europe hasn't reached out to the US with boldness since. Their own markets work fine, thank you.

Since then, the XC trade has seemed focused on high-margin race gear and avoiding PR.

Regional Recovery?

Despite a calamitous past, and the snowbike boom, and today's thinner snow, skiing *is* growing and 100,000 skis sold ain't chopped liver.

We still have a good dozen skiing hotspots nationwide — like the Methow Valley in WA — and several major events, especially the Birkebeiner, which balloons a little northwoods town from 2,000 to 30,000 for a weekend each winter.

In our hotspots, we have youth leagues, high school teams and college programs. And adult ski clubs.

There are still a few Nordic shops and online stores, and a few big box chains still sell XC.

It's a solid little scene. But the loss of widespread snow country infrastructure explains why few today seem to know how amazing modern XC is. And is it replacing itself as it ages? ...Only in those few hotspots.

Radically Casual

Nowadays, encouraging skiing to be done simply anywhere there's snow using rugged everyday type gear would be a radical act. Skiing is one big family, but the establishment doesn't care enough about casual skiing to promote it even though it must be the most common. Also, unplugging the experience from the resorts would be radical. It would be resented as a betrayal of those who've invested in the sport for generations. Asserting that anyone can just go out and track-in their own worldclass ski experience is radical. But ski liberation will require going beyond the usual influencers. The key is going to be celebrating the joy of local trails and even roadtrips will need to embrace low overhead action.

You're Special!

If you are new to skiing I think there are several special things about you worth noting. You're probably not getting into skiing thanks to a groomed course racer-type who you know. It's also not likely that you saw the gear at a shop, nor did you notice any PR for the sport.

You are stepping out on your own, or with the help of friends who are unaffiliated with official mainstream skiing. You will have very few options for help so you will likely develop your skills on your own. You are one of very few new skiers. You won't have many others you can look to. If you do interact with official skiers there's a strong chance you'll come away confused. These are real barriers. It can only help to be aware of them.

Give yourself all the props for finding this sport and please do not be discouraged. Right now it's word of mouth. But the help and fun that you can relate to are out there. However, you might have to make it up on your own as you go. You might have to click a lot or drive far to find gear. And if you find a shop that sells a little XC on the side, the staff might not know what they are doing. This is a golden age for outdoor sport -- for skiing, too -- but not for the ski market. The market and its supports (or lack thereof) right now is simply not conducive to you. Of course, there still are great shops, resorts

and instructors and helpful media. In some ways things are much better. In other ways, the scene is much, much smaller than it was or than it should be, and it has been needlessly complexified -- and not by me. Thankfully there are work-arounds. Gumption is part of it. You've actually qualified as exceptional by getting this far. Keep trying and you'll get there. It can be so much fun! (And the fact that you're daring to read this book, ha! You're a goner!)

Singletrack is alluring. And skis love any kind of snow. What more do we need?

The Skate Divide

The advent of skate-skiing brought a watershed moment, which was not well-handled. Bill Koch didn't deliver gold at the Olympics but a short time later he launched in a whole new side to the sport to the world: he showed us how to skate.

Skating was fast and fun and you didn't have to worry about kickwax in tricky situations -- which are unfortunately common.

According to ski media leaders I've spoken to, as well as my own experience, skating divided the sport and confused the culture with no leadership rising up to sort it out, explain or sell it. People thought they had to quit what they'd been doing. The new style promised speed but without leadership or coaching, casual skiers thought the new speed required an outlandishly higher level of fitness. Skating also required wider trails and more expensive grooming. Indeed, it required grooming. Where grooming used to be a pleasing extra, now one couldn't even enjoy skiing unless you had access to a trail system where the club had been able to afford $100k in machinery. And now instead of having one set of trusty gear, one needed two sets. At first, enthusiasts simply abandoned classic skiing. In the first decade of skating, classic was dropped, ignored, looked down on. Casual, social skiers by the thousands were alienated and fell away. Events abruptly became skating-only and lost the big casual "iceberg" portion of their entries. Ski events transitioned from social outings to purely athletic. From there, as waxing intensified, it swung into the even more exotic strata of athlete-technician.

At first even racers didn't know how to skate. ...Let that sink in. Skating changed the sport yet we could hardly skate up a hill. Extra effort was indeed required. The everyman spirit of XC faded. Some events grew, but granola was cast aside in favor of the Powerbar and heart-rate monitor. What's more, skating cost more to get gear of an enjoyable quality. I've heard from top brass that "skating killed skiing."

A decade after skating took over, a secret emerged that classic skiing was still being done half the time by the world's elites, even though there weren't any classic events. It was lower impact, higher tempo. What's more, they liked it. It became clear that both forms used nearly the same technique, energy and dynamics. They were completely complimentary.

We calmed down and realized that skating was only 10% faster, and that some courses were favorable to classic, and skating wasn't harder, and singletrack loved only classic.

But a full realization that "all skiing is one" has never been promoted. BC is little known to groomed skiers. However, the recovery of classic is a move in the right direction.

Classic races became part of annual schedules again. Today they comprise half the events. And nearly every event has categories for the "other side." However, the emphasis on elite racing endures. The sport has never regained respect for its mellow majority or its singletrack skills.

Let's Rescue Our Climate!

Climate change sucks. We're losing snow. But we don't have to take it sitting down. The best thing we can do is start enjoying winter if we're not and to keep skiing if we already know how.

Skiers are awesome bellwethers for this disaster. We can be witnesses and reporters for what is happening. Those who play outside will be in the best position to easily adapt to the changes that will be needed to keep the earth functioning. But we still need to cut back on burning fuel. So we need to embrace local-first. And we need to accept reality by bundling up and being more active in winter. So we can tolerate cooler furnace settings. And we need to relax more in the heat of summer while using less AC.

In the meantime, there are LOTS of ways to keep skiing in low snow!

Winter Whining -- Ugh!

Something has happened to the good cheer of the USA in winter: It has become acceptable to moan about it. Maybe more people can afford to flee the cold. Boomers from the Midwest become annual Snowbirds migrating south.

This bad attitude is part of a huge health crisis. Michigan in particular has poor health. You might think winter is kind of short and you can get by with winter-hate by switching to gym time indoors. Well, a lot of people don't have that time or money. Avoiding fresh air for any amount of time is a bad idea. We need sunlight in winter more than any other time of year.

Most people who say they don't like winter simply are more idle then, and gain weight once it's cold. And most never lose it all again. I think our general public being more idle for a few months each year is a significant cause of obesity and sickness. It locks in the toxic persistence of sedentary lifestyles. Winter is not expendable! Outdoor activity in winter is not optional!

In the Potential chapter I'll show you ways to fall in love with snow if you live in snow country!

Lame-Ass Stereotypes

In the USA, skiing is strategically identified with luxury, which is reasonable since a day on the slopes can be crazy expensive and has been designed to involve travel

and lodging since not many of us actually live near big hills or mountains.

XC skiing is identified with hippies, retirees, nerds and fitness freaks, which is ridiculous. But the stereotypes don't stop there. And none of this is part of intentional marketing, since XC has none.

XC is subjected to the lamest PR stereotypes – and they all need to be defeated, called out, and efforts made in the direction of reality and our many obvious positives if XC is going to recover.

Ski Liberation!

Let's liberate skiing! Let's take a look at skiing unplugged, skiing with no strings attached. But since all skiing is fine, anything you ever want to add onto it is fine, too. I'm going to show you my take about where it starts. And I'll show a way that delivers the biggest part to the most people. I'll show you the cake … and a lot of the

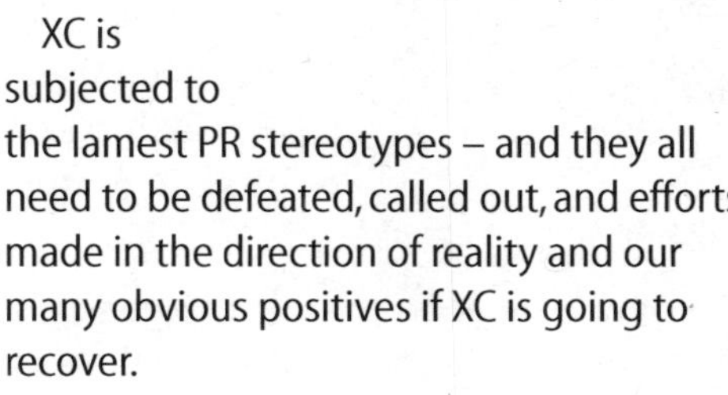

Stan, finishing an awesome singletrack outing with a bunch of friends. It snowed, we spread the word, gathered the next day, and hit it. Nowadays you have to carpe diem. Stan is a top-shelf mt-biker, trail-runner, and organizer of super-fun trail ski events. (Check the 40-yr-old skis!)

Cyclocross Worlds in the US drew 10k fans in icy "bad snow" conditions. Skiers can similarly learn to relish the handling challenges of technical courses in tricky weather. (photo T. Potter)

icing. Skiing is a big tent!

A big thing is that XC today is like roadbiking was in the late 1980's, all tight clearances and super thin rockhard tires that were only good on perfect pavement. Then mountain biking showed up with its fun and versatility and blew people's minds. That's what trail skiing offers XC today -- a way to break free from being bound to grooming. Want a breakthrough? It's yours for the taking!

A new generation of thrifty, rugged, versatile gear has come out -- and the world is full of trails. They're everywhere and they're free! Fields, forests and frozen waterways are often covered in snow in winter. It's all there for you! Ride the wave!

Let's add more fun, too. That will bust skiing out of its current seriousness and let normal people relate to it again — all of it. (Like, skating is something we can all have fun with. It's not for "fitness" or "racing.") Normalization is a thing. It's finally happening in the US with bikes. Next up, XC.

The Mt-Bike of Skis

The mt-bike of skis has arrived! Skiing trails with these mt-bike-like skis is the future! ...MTB > MTXC!

Actually, this set-up has been here awhile now, but the ski industry doesn't sell it very hard or as the solution to easy skiing or a way to put XC on the rebound. So if you request this at a ski shop they actually won't know what you're talking about -- yet! But if you explain it, they'll catch on!

The mt-bike of skiing is the combo of a pivoting cuff BC touring boot, a BC binding, and a midlength, midwidth nowax ski. This rig delivers great handling, liveliness, stability and control. Awesome for exploring most any trail, especially steeper and more technical singletrack. Set-tracks and grooming are no longer required! Throw in groovy tele turns on a whim!

Thanks to the many technical advances embodied in this new set-up, the learning curve for skiing today is shorter than ever and delivers more handling joy.

Mt-bikers are an awesome, untapped demographic for XC skiing. They can relate to the nimble versatility of this new equipment and THEY LOVE SKIING THE TRAILS THEY RIDE! ...And that's why our motto is: "Ski What You Ride."

Ironically, groomed-course skiers are proving to be the least likely of all groups to try trail skiing. We find mt-bikers to be the most eager. "Serious" skiers are addicted to grooming. They're more likely to fatbike a snowtrail than ski it! Roadbikers are conservative, but they are usually open-minded enough to also mt-bike.

Not so with serious Nordic skiers! They're rarely willing to try the mt-bike of skis on singletrack, but we think they'd like if they did! It might be that they've just never experienced the control of this new set-up. Skiing trails with their usual gear would be daunting, but if they gave the new way a try...

Snowbikes – the Elephant in the Room

Yes, many riders are snowbiking on their fatbikes these days come winter, but the appeal of skiing's simplicity and change-of-pace action, variety and healthy cross-training is still strong.

Fatbikes are now the main winter thing in many places, especially low snow parts of the north country. They're a great solution to low snow. Skiing hasn't done much to challenge this. The issue needs to be dealt with. It's not simple and there are many interesting aspects, all with ripe chances for skiing.

Who is building and grooming new singletrack snow trail, and innovating new snow groomers? ...Fatbikers! They are leading the way, with support from runners and snowshoers. Skiers aren't hardly in the conversation, except to holler "NIMBY"! (How much new ski trail is being built? Microscopic! We still have a lot of our heritage ski trails, established in the 60's-70's, and still laid out to those specs.)

Like most skiers, I love biking. No need to pretend these are separate worlds. I

give full props to the snowtrail work the fatties are leading! I've tried fatties and I appreciate that with a $5k carbon fatty I can get regular mt-bike-type performance on hardpack snow. They're also great for marginal conditions, and reducing impact, but I'm just not into using one skillset and range-of-motion all year. Though I see occasions when they're awesome.

Also, there's something to the idea that bikes are still machines while a ski is elemental -- basically just a stick, like a paddle or a bow. This is cool.

Learning from Bikes

There's been a global boom in several new kinds of biking and bike culture along

We do a lot of trail-sharing in our local multi-use trail scene. Everyone is invited on our outings, provided they know the basics of playing nice.

Fun at the Women's Ski Tour in Traverse City. Take away the "hardcore," add some party = people show up!

Cost matters! As a kid I rarely could afford to do downhill skiing, but once I had XC skis I could ski for free anywhere and every day there was snow!

The outdoor liberation movement of the 60's had a big DIY thrift component. XC marketing has since moved away from that. I'll move it back.

Snow falls on everyone and makes for a good party. It's equal opportunity. When the XC scene moves beyond the Type-A tech-geekery of affluent old white guys ... and into a normal range of fun and culture, it'll appeal to a much wider range of demographics.

with a celebration of everyday biking, including bike fashion. Bike parties, cyclocross, bikepacking, enduro -- these are significant changes that happened after the last time XC had any big changes. Each of them has something the ski scene can learn from.

Ski Justice

Ever since skiing has become less popular I've noticed a widening gap between its official culture and how average people ski, or might ski if they were ever shown how simple it is.

Skiing needs to be inclusive before it can move up. It needs to add pathways for affordability and access. Kids, women and minorities of all kinds and incomes need to know that in XC they have a winter home for fun, warm, gliding around everywhere there's snow.

Ladies in the Lead

I was inspired to add party to our local ski scene thanks to the Women's Ski Tour that Kaye Kraypohl and her friends started in Traverse City, MI, in 1999. She was a top racer but saw the sport struggling to attract more than a dozen women in her area, even though it was a winter hot-spot. She decided to host a fun event for women. The first year 200 showed up. Within a couple years it was thousands. It wasn't that women didn't like skiing: they wanted the kind that was fun. The WST featured chocolate, wine and party tents along the ski trail. It dropped the "serious" attitude and raised money for a women's shelter. Win-win-win. Inspired, I started trying to spread a fun-first approach where I lived.

Outdoor Underground

An indicator of social health is if a scene has alternatives, a counterculture. Biking has long had this in a wide variety. For awhile in the 1970's XC skiing had it, too. (Free your heel, free your mind.) XC is green, DIY, and sustainable. Casual trail skiing has no mediation, it's direct action. There's no middleman. It's a mode of authentic outdoor experience. When skate-skiing arrived skiing swung hard away from the cosmic side to an elite ultra-niche athlete identity, leaving any alternative style off its map. What would that look like now? We wouldn't know...

To date there has been one counterculture ski book: Hal Painter's "The Cross Country Ski Cook, Look & Pleasure Book." It was influential. It came out in the late 70's, expressing an ultra 70's view, then was totally eclipsed by the performance mentality it lampooned. Why, here was a ski book that included a woman's voice, sex, nudity, zen, yogurt, and marijuana! …All the ways that many skiers lived in real life, but the market pretended didn't exist.

We need direct-action winter outdoor fun to stay connected to what's really out there. This book confirmed for me the idea that outdoor sport was a big tent and could be part of a lifelong effort

toward liberation and friendships. (I got the reprint rights and also sold originals for years.)

I've had people tell me that the lack of alternatives in a scene means the public is happy the way things are. One size fits all. Skiing is ignored because people don't like it, get over it. …Well, I don't buy it!

The Reverend Lester Polyester outpacing a few of his rivals back in the day.

The 80's were a heady era. As a lycra juggernaut swept o'er the land, a few, a merry few, rose up and made gestures of skewering the new sacred cows.

Coincidentally, at this time on other trails far away I decided that a red cotton union suit was a suitable parody of a lycra ski-suit and entered races wearing that ... and a coonskin hat.

Thanks to the Rev for his inspiration and advice in the confabulation of this book!

Culture: Cross Country Potential

In the previous chapter I set out the situation that XC skiing seems to find itself in, at least in what seems to me like a big part of the USA. In light of all that, where can we take this sport? Well, why not start with…

How would a kid like to ski? Take a kid…and snow…what next?

Getting ready for the Fire & Ice Relay Race Party.

This idea contains the secret to democratizing the sport. …It snows, you make a fun place for skiing that is as close as possible to the kids and everyone else. That means city parks. Of whatever size. Use the terrain like a kid would. You have a park with some hills? Loop a course up, down and around those suckas.

At this point it seems like a huge majority of the public simply doesn't know about XC. This includes people who bike and do other outdoor fun. And if they do say they know about it, they have outrageously wrong ideas. All these people still seem like our best base for recruiting. We have to get to a wide level of realistic public awareness to have any hope of a generalized winter-love breakthrough.

Pay to Play

What's the best way to get to where we need to be? Let's start with the big picture and the next generation. And let's see if this idea sticks…If you feel a little discomfort, it might be working…

The hook'n'bullet'n'powersports worlds have a huge amount of access, resources, respect and youth education. Why? …I suggest it's because they pay. …With licenses and excise tax.

If fresh-air lifelong outdoor rec wants some of that, would like to be a real part of our world, and have our kids learn about glide, reality and health, we'll have to start shopping. It's time to buy some culture … and the resources that support it. Yeah, we already pay trail pass in some places. We need more.

Adapting to Climate Change

However, for right here and now, for this coming ski season, if you want to ski as often as possible, as easily as possible, that means figuring how to enjoy skiing on LESS SNOW. Because that's the present-day situation in most snow-country.

Thankfully, there are easy ways to do this!

As it is, in snow country, when there's

any snow (I mean *in fact*, even if you don't think it's there) -- you can ski as easily as you can go to a gym.

There are at least five ways to deal with sketchier snow levels.

(How often does such strategizing come up in today's how-to-ski info? Rarely. Astonishing.)

The current efforts seem to be about the big picture. That's dire for sure, unless the world changes. In the meantime, I'm gonna ski. And so can everybody else.

...And I'm gonna ski sustainably as best I can. Smallest footprint for the mostest skiing.

The solutions our local gang has figured out are as follows: *Ski on thinner snow. *Travel to snow -- doesn't always have to be farther, just a different direction. *Ski on manmade snow. *Plan to quickly change when and where you go to get that snow. *Diversify.

(The following chapter gets into the details.)

All Snow is Good Snow

Skiing's natural situation is: when there is snow, you can have fun skiing.

Yes, this is beautiful. But it's a bit like a road. It's awesome for road-type skiing. I suggest that we also consider the lovely curves of all the hiking and biking trails out there as we play and promote our fun in all the places we get snow.

I mean frozen ground. Once we have frost in the ground we can get a little iciness on top, a skimcoat, and then a bit of snow here and there will make a base and start to add up. Suddenly you have a compacted inch over the leaves on your favorite mt-bike trail ... and you can ski!

Yes, leaves might become more a part of your ski life. Usually you can just ignore them. ... Or enjoy them! Autumn leaves are pretty in, on and under snow. Whenever our gang is skiing in thin slush we're mesmerized by the beauty of the red and yellow leaves glowing through the translucent snow. Indeed, there can be more ooh's and aah's at such times than when out on just plain snow.

You don't need much snow: all skis need is enough to glide. (Any more than that, they don't care. What do they know? As long as they can glide, they're happy!)

Can you believe, I know skiers in our town who'll tell me there wasn't enough snow to ski at all locally last year when I got out 50 times.

So the snow is sometimes an hour away rather than 10 minutes. Or maybe it's manmade snow at an alpine area. Or maybe you'll have to change the outing to Sunday rather than Saturday to catch a fickle weather system passing through. Once you have a bit of snow, somewhere near, you're good!

Here's a little quote. My friend Dave relates the following: "Chris Stoppel once told me as I pondered a sketchy drop at Mount Bohemia before they put lifts on it: 'Dave, all snow is good snow, all hills are good hills, and all skis are rock skis.' Then he kicked the snowy build-up off his red

kick-waxed alpine skis and proceeded to drop a knee." Says it all.

...And All Skis are Rock Skis

Skiers today often complain they can't ski local low snow because they don't have "rock skis." Firstly, they don't have rock skis because they're being overly focused and specialized and only have one kind of ski, basically. But mostly they're looking at the situation backwards. If they're going to live here then their skis should reflect their available skiing. Instead we end up with the situation of most skiers not skiing much, and never on the funnest casual local trails. (I don't think they could even measure the effect scratches have on their speed, but an uber-Type-A often loathes imperfection.) Really, skis that are suitable for skiing around here are just skis. If we're enthusiasts we'll have a variety of skis. But they're all skis. No need to say "rock."

If Nordic devotees give trail skiing a try they might see that they can like a wider range of skiing ... and enjoy a wider range of snow, which is what climate change brings. The upside is ... a wider range of snow!

Skinny vs Powerful

It's true that skinny people have it easier going up hills. It's easier for them to acquire a big power to weight ratio. But if we're not racing as long as we're getting pay-off, we're good.

Powerful, stocky people often prefer gravity-fed speed, airtime, and downwardness. They're great with resisting the

Skiing the ungroomed singletrack Potawatomi trail in Michigan delivers supreme flow even though it's "oldschool" singletrack. It rewards expert ski handling skills and a zesty attitude.

G-forces of high-speed turns with maximum ski carving and flex. They can absorb the hits from big air landings and mishaps. Thankfully, an up-track doesn't care how long you take to tromp it. ...Or you can live near chairlifts.

XC skiing hasn't ever had a Clydesdale weight division for some reason -- this might be another example of skiing already having dropped so far in relevance that it didn't notice other sports adopting the concept.

The powerhouse demographic might well be finding a comfy new home in fatbiking, a non-weight-bearing sport which seems to be welcoming all comers without any elitist tendency.

Nowax: the Ticket to Low-Snow

Nowax skis today come in the usual fish-scale patterns, but there also several new high-tech options, like the "skin" skis with fuzzy grip or the "zero" skis with rubbery grip. These glide better and are quieter than fishscales. To me they seem like the future. But so far they are only promoted in the racing lines.

Personally, I've really been enjoying new old-stock Blizzard "Chemical" skis, the one wider touring model I've found with the "zero" rubbery grip. Here's hoping that ski companies soon make these types of features fully available in their ski models that are more suitable to average skiers on today's low-snow!

Nowax of any type is also the preferred option when a day is likely to warm up above freezing even if it's going to get cooler later. It can be hard to kickwax for such weather, often requiring stopping and rewaxing several times as the weather changes, but nowax grip patterns don't care and will keep working no matter what.

Whenever you're in a region, or even in a time of winter, where temperatures will stay reliably below zero during the day with minor fluctuation then kickwax gives easily best results. When daily temps range from 10degF to 20degF and back again, you're in the sweet spot. Such conditions often happen for a few weeks each season even in fickle areas so waxable skis are good to keep around. The weeks when you can wax Blue or Extra-Blue and just leave it on the skis from day to day are among the most wonderful. (Well, all kinds of ski conditions have their strongpoints to cherish.) But when temps swing through a similar range but from 25 to 35 and back you'd need to change wax several times. (Sometimes skiing terrain that has a combination of sunny parts and shady parts can have a similar effect even at somewhat colder temps.) Then nowax comes on strong.

The Ready-for-Everything Quiver

At the same time, ski buffs who want to enjoy the few supreme snowfalls that they get each season might end up with a "quiver" of differing skis, each designed for special conditions. The upshot of using different kinds of skis is that the wear'n'tear of even low-snow conditions is distributed among them and the various sets might last many more years than usual.

Seeing Snow

Outdoor buffs today might often say their home area has no snow or "bad snow." These places often actually have plenty of snow if you know where to look or how to ski.

You need to find where your less snow is the most! In regions where snow is fickle the wind and sun will still usually leave more snow in some places than in others. South-facing areas might lose snow the same day it falls while shady forests and north-facing terrain might hold and even accumulate snow. Find those places where you live!

Where I live I have a favorite 20-acre woodlot of glaciated terrain next to 80 acres of hilly golf course. In the past the course was groomed for skiing and for local people still ski it, even though the grooming stopped decades ago. This area is subject to arctic gales and the full brunt of whatever sun we get. It is often terrible. However, because it's wide-open the very few local people who skate-ski will struggle to track in a course. When we do get snow any trail-making drifts in immediately. If the temperature warms a bit it turns to grass in a day. But… right next door in the forest I have laid out a couple miles of supreme flow-trail singletrack that holds snow better than anywhere else around. While terrible conditions come and go in the open area, with sometimes zero actually pleasant conditions, the shady forest usually offers wonderful skiing every day. So, we just need to pick the right place and the right way to ski!

Then there's spring skiing. Even in a low-snow winter, snowfalls can keep happening in spring, giving supreme quality skiing in gentle temps. So don't put away your skis too soon! Keep grabbing what you can!

Take Care of Your Trails & Your Bod

When you don't get much snow it's important that everyone in your community is on the same page about trail care. If it's slushy one day and someone goes out and flounders their way around the trail for Lord knows what reason experiencing who knows what kind of misery and the forecast is for a hard freeze for the next week then that one screw-up can wreck the trail for all users after that. This is especially true if there was only a few inches of snow on the ground during the thaw.

Slush "splashes" then freezes and impedes walkers, runners, skiers, bikers -- everybody. So when the slush is on, trailworkers should put out signs at trailheads saying something like "Trail Closed to All Use Due to Slush." Or "Do No Harm -- do not leave marks in trail that will freeze and impair future use."

Mt-bikers today know to avoid "pizza cutting" and to use 3"+ wide tires run at pressures that don't leave marks deeper than a 1/2" or so. ...And not to ride when conditions are bad for it.

Other vital trail care for stretching your fun in low snow is to make sure sticks and stones are picked up. A trail can be short-mowed turf, requiring only a little frost and snow to be enjoyable. When cared for right a trail only needs to be frozen with about an inch on top for good skiing. Even frozen, icy leaves can help improve a base.

Now, a downside of low snow and frozen ground is more pain when crashing. You have to be more careful not to get hurt. Wearing protection is sensible compared to when there's a foot of cushy powder on top of a nice base to catch you.

Sexy. Slush. Like a cyclocross tire in mud that's translucent. Skis love glide wherever it can be found.

Heading out for a Waterloo Epic at oh-dark-thirty. 36 miles of gloriously glaciated backcountry singletrack trail-breaking on this popular regional hiking trail network. Not skied end-to-end by anyone but our gang, that we know. We got a kick'n'glide groove going that we got deeper and deeper into.

It's easy to get harsh bruises and bloody scrapes when crashing on an inch of icy snow over frozen ground. We've started wearing mt-bike shorts with hip padding and football forearm thin-pads and knee-guards...even a bike helmet. ....Whatever works! It also depends on your personal crash tendencies. Some hit their knees, some never do. Some have bony butts, some have more of nature's padding

Liberate Lunch-hour!

Keep your skis in the car and stay ready! Be prepared to squeeze your weekday lunch-hours. This is good for you anyway. Get outside during the week in daylight as much as you can. It greatly increases your chances of good snow. And it boosts your sun exposure. You ski and ski-party with friends so you're good on S.A.D. already but everything helps.

Night Time is the Right Time

If the only time it cools down enough is at night then why not opt for night skiing! Night is great for a group, for an event, as well as for solo fun. You can use trail lighting, or get your headlamps running. There are a jillion varieties of headlamp out there: make sure yours casts a wide, even, white flood pattern and that it has a remote battery pack that you can tuck under your jacket to optimize your awesome new LiPo power-source, since cold kills batteries, and make sure its run-time matches your use need. (Bring a spare battery in case.)

With short daylight hours and awesome, affordable headlight technology there's no reason to avoid the night. Before and after work are now completely viable ski times.

Consider the temps, though. Snow temp lags behind the air as it cools and can take a couple hours to get good again.

Maybe today doesn't have enough snow and you have to work tomorrow but a good snowfall is forecast in the evening. Another good reason for a night ski. Be ready to go whenever the time is right!

Lighted trails are fairly common. You could help your community park make that happen. Skiers can pull a sled around a loop to set out rechargeable LED lights or solar lights or liquid fuel lamps of whatever kind. You could also fundraise to erect a string of elevated seasonal electrical lighting. Trail-lights mesh nicely with headlamps.

Winter is not the only thing to give your local landscape new vistas and appearance. Night brings its own refreshing change, turning the familiar into an adventure.

...And a night ski segues smoothly into apres' ski R&R at a nearby "ski lodge" pub.

Culture: Thriving in Climate Change

Let's further explore solutions to the problem of unreliable snow that I listed in the previous chapter...

This is a huge topic for skiing. But if we handle it right we might be able to ski MORE today than we used to.

Climate change is the biggest thing that skiing has to contend with. Yeah, we're going to lose places to ski. Many will have to drive more or move. But there is, and will be, a whole lot of middle ground and, still, a whole lot of snow, even though it's appearance will change.

What does it mean if our skiable days drop from, say, 75 a season to 50? Sure, that's bad, but isn't the main question what we do with the 50?

The most important thing in this new era will be if the public gets outside experiencing the reality of where they live. And doesn't back down. And if we let others know what's happening. Winter-haters tend to cheer at the news of warm winter days. They need to be shut down. ...I mean educated. Because of our experience as skiers we're better able to do the right thing and cut back on fossil fuels. And we won't fall for the sucker-lines the billion-

aire energy-sellers throw at us.

I'm already hearing the dirge talk about the loss of skiing. However, I have yet to see anyone but our little gang stand up for the many easy ways of continuing to ski on less snow.

There is no reason to give up skiing just because winters are "worse"!

Actually, scarcity enhances appreciation. Absence makes the heart grow. Having fewer times to ski makes those times more special not less.

Do people who like things like scuba

Recent winters have bounced between extremes. A local brewpub sponsored our Fire & Ice Relay Party one "good" winter of extreme cold. Three microbrews sponsored our events. ...Did you know that microbrews have fewer chances for PR in winter? Our Ski Party knows!

Bikers are leading the latest R&D for singletrack grooming and playing on trails. Would it be fun if skiers joined them? Here's the cutting-edge US "Best Tracksled" stand-behind pulling groomer, based on the Russian Snowdog. There are many ways to use this sled.

diving expect to do it a lot in order to like it?

For most of us all our skiing is affected somehow by lower snow levels. We've already looked a lot of ways adapting to less snow can help us optimize our ski scene. But there's even more we can do.

First, Let's Defeat Warming!

First, to defeat climate change we need to switch over to sustainable energy sources. And we need to change how we live. Eat less factory food, especially meat. Drive less, fly less. Be warm in the summer, wear more in the winter. If the USA led the way, other countries might follow.

Yeah, that's a biggie. In the meantime...

Ski on Less Snow!

Do you ever wonder if it's possible to ski on low snow? Wonder how much is really needed to ski? To get all the glide and control you need? The answer is as I've said: all you need is frozen ground with an inch packed and another inch for frosting.

In low-snow conditions it really helps to have trails that have been cared-for: sticks picked up, stones kicked out. In this way with the least possible snow you can still have great skiing.

Specifically, to enjoy low-snow skiing,

you need to stop babying your ski bases. And you need skis built for durability. These are usually mid-range skis which are labeled as intermediate in quality level. But for the needs of low-snow trail skiing, these are now advanced, elite skis! Featherweight "air" skis are too fragile and get demoted for thin snow. (Is a roadbike "advanced" for riding singletrack or is a mt-bike what you want?)

Harden-up Your Attitude to Skis

As snow becomes thinner, we really will scratch our skis more. Let's accept it!

I scratch my skis all the time but do not notice any effect. We probably shouldn't be very concerned about scratches.

Very rarely, I'll gouge a ski deeply enough that I want to repair it maybe once every 10 years. To do so, we just use a P-Tex candle made of base material that we light, drip into the gouge, then sand smooth.

Nowax fishscale patterns can get worn away from skiing over roots and rocks and lose their grip, so that's a thing. We refresh them by slicing with a box-cutter or X-acto knife to make fresh rearward-facing "scales"!

Skis don't spoil. They have no freshness dating. Whether you go out 5 or 20 times a season, skis don't care. Skis should be considered slow-wearing consumables. If you ski a little they can hang out for decades. If you ski a lot they might last 5-10 years for waxers, 3-5 for nowax.

Either way, we shouldn't begrudge our skis' lifespans. If having wonderful low-snow ski experiences means that a $200 pair lasts 3 years rather than 4, we should be happy to amortize that fun.

Wouldn't it be nice if ski-makers tried to improve our predicament by making bases (and cambers) more wear-resistant?

You'll want to be able to easily boss your skis to glide smoothly over any sticks or dry spots you might encounter: so bring on the mt-bike of skis! ...Metal edges on a mid-length ski with a pivot-cuff boot and stout BC binding let us easily enjoy very varied terrain and a wide range of conditions. Be safe and stable even when it's sketchy and grabby! Slushy leaves, sticks and roots are part of today's snowsport. Indeed, a variety of things in the trail are interesting to look at as you ski along. Just step around any problems.

Travel to Find Snow!

Really, this usually doesn't involve that much more travel. Yes, we prefer to ski in our neighborhoods, but often we have to drive to a trail, just like mt-biking. It might just be in a different direction than what you're used to.

The snow was an hour to the east but that melted and now it's an hour to the west. No biggie!

Sure, whole regions can suffer total melt-off's, but snow usually returns within a week to some zone that may well be only an hour further away than you're used to, if that.

And your local snow might leave early. Unseasonably warm temps often see us biking again in March. But an hour or two north, it's still ski season! Again: don't put away your skis! Sure, start riding. But catching that juicy corn snow is a good idea.

It doesn't help to impede the popularity of skiing by arbitrarily insisting on an overly tight proximity range, or predictability. People drive for all their hobbies, so let's not hold XC to a different standard.

Make winter driving awesome rather than stressful by swapping in a sweet set of snow tires.

Build up a carpool party. Maybe even buy a club van! More friends increases the fun and reduces the impact.

Ski on Manmade Snow!

Snowmaking requires a fan and a water hose. Yeah, some high-tech, too, but it's not that intense. Google says the cost is $70-2000/acre, with snowguns $500-$5k. Let's see more!

Of course, there already is a lot of snowmaking – at downhill ski areas. Let's make deals with them to let us ski around the margins of their slopes. Maybe we could create optimized Nordic courses using the margins of the base areas, making mile-long loops. Special parts of slopes could be set aside and crafted to be more conducive to the handling traits of XC skis. Sure, others could still ski or board on these portions but there might be features XC skiers would especially like. Perhaps we could see terrain parks for XC. Can all snowsport play together? It seems at least as likely as the other big recent changes to ski areas.

World Cup skiing relies on man-made snow. Maybe some of this can trickle down to everyday skiers.

Some XC ski resorts now also feature snowmaking. But so far I've seen it located where it's easiest to make and handle the resulting snow -- like a small, simple oval loop. Such set-ups seem suited for the bare rudiments, not for increasing XC popularity.

Instead, let's aim our snowmaking cannons over a compact yet still awesome course! Or use a shorter snow-spreading trailer that can handle banked and off-camber turns.

Cyclocross and skateboard are done in tiny urban parks. Alpine terrain parks are compact. C'mon, Nordic, let's get with it!

I don't necessarily mean the Nordix or Nordicross that we've seen. Such courses seems to result in floundering and splatting. Maybe if the gear used was more robust it would be fine. Who knows what a fun, challenging, compact course would look like if designed in light of Nordic skills?

Remember, the greater control of much of today's XC gear means we don't need set-tracks. We have more options now.

Moveable Feast! —Plan Light to Change Quick

The interconnected overhead of today's ski establishment doesn't mesh well at all with low snow and unpredictable conditions. Fragile skis require grooming which requires expensive equipment which requires big entry fees. It all means deep snow, deep pockets and elaborate planning. As a result an ever-more limited demographic of people participate in skiing and disappointment is ever more common.

The flipside is to design the skiing around your likely snow conditions.

The "moveable feast" comes from Hemingway's writing about Paris in the 1920's: people had rewarding cultural fun for little money because they were willing to change things up. They lived in attics, and for summer fun they'd go backpacking. In winter it was hut to hut ski-touring. A lot of famous modern art was made in this low overhead way. They stretched their dollars while living a bohemian version of luxury. That's my take on it, anyway.

Skiing in an age of fickle weather benefits from a footloose attitude.

Let's plan, but just don't fixate on the location. Or even the date.

Be ready to go anywhere within reason to find the snow. Prepare the same as you would in every other respect, but if a change of venue is needed to find the snow, put the word out and everyone goes to the new place.

Or keep the original location but have a rain (snow) date a day or week later. Weather systems can be staggered by as little as a day or by a hundred miles. Rely on a communication-tree rather than rigid plans.

Yes, you might have to forego reservations and this in turn might impinge on event insurance, so we might have to switch to unofficial status! Relations with park managers might need to be developed to find a way to handle rain-dates and changes of venue. They're trying to adapt to climate change as well! Together we have to adapt to thrive!

If events were simpler we could have twice as many, in twice as many locations, each with two dates.

If you skip grooming and things like electronic chip timing then it's easier to quickly change a venue.

Another factor you can play with is time of day. Nowadays good snow can be separated from slop by mere hours. If a warmup is going to happen, be nimble enough to move your ski time to earlier in the day while it's still cool. Or plan around mornings to begin with. If temps are wandering above and below freezing in a day, build in the flexibility to grab the best conditions. Don't get frustrated: be prepared to change!

Round-Robin Scheduling

We call our local ski gang the Funhogs. The Southeast Michigan Fun Hogs, to be exact. Or, the SeMiFuHos, when texting. We bike, boat, XC ski, tele ski, party year-round. We casually created the MI XC BC Series of a half dozen trail events. We've been evolving it as we deal with climate change.

We started by planning one event per month then bumping it to the next weekend if no snow. The weather sometimes foils even that approach. We have snowy weekends without an event along with events that miss both of their dates.

Our latest idea is to start the next new year having an event planned for each weekend. If they all go off, great. We just start at the beginning again the next open weekend and we'll have an outing every weekend there's snow. But if we lose

a weekend due to no snow that event bumps to the end of the line.

Diversify! Skiing is Just One Piece of the Snow Season Puzzle

Skiing isn't the only way to enjoy winter. We are people, not "skiers." It's not like 30 miles of skiing is always better than 20 miles or 10. Quantity isn't everything. If the snow is icy hard but softens up to give perfect ski conditions, say, at 10 a.m., hit the trails then and ski the heck out of the awesomeness you find. But if it's going to get sunny and sloppy by noon, don't fret, just shift your winter fun over to another fresh air experience!

Like, put canoes on the river and enjoy paddling the crystal clear waters of winter

Bike racing has long embraced intentionally adverse "bad" conditions. Technical courses in compact areas are great for spectating and socializing. ...Similarly, XC skiing can learn how to make wonderful lemons from its low-snow lemonade!

If winter reduces one of our favorite things we don't throw up our hands and quit. Nor does it mean that we obsess and plan around a few big-ticket far-away rarified experiences – that could be ruined by an overnight rainshower.

We build a way to experience skiing and winter around the best chances and fun activities that fit with the kind of snow experience we find closest and most reliably. If unpredictability is today's predictable, then we create with that in mind.

Layne had the great idea for us to combine a day of paddling downstream on the world-famous AuSable river followed by 12 miles of skiing back along the riverbanks on the Mason Tract trail. It was an awesome combo outing during a warmer winter when the river didn't freeze. We used it as an opportunity to have a richer experience!

with snowy riverbanks. You could drop boats upstream before breakfast then go ski up to the boats then paddle back down to the cars.

Or, maybe you've lost most of your snow. Ski it while it's good then head over to an interesting lake covered in ice and do some Nordic Skating using your ski boots and poles! Some of our favorite waterways have complex shorelines that lets us ice skate for miles feeling like we're still in the forest. …. Set some ice-fishing tip-ups out along the way! Catch your dinner by the time you finish your first lap. … Thus the bonfire. Camp out! If it's a mild winter, all the easier for your enjoyment of some crystal clear winter skies.

Hardly any of us are "just skiers." Misguided marketing thinks we put all our eggs in one basket. Nearly all of us are bikers, paddlers, wanderers, campers. … These can all be part of the ski experience!

Culture: Earnin' Your Turns

I enjoy downhill skiing, but for decades I never put downhill and XC together. I had downhill in a separate box that included chairlifts (with their limitations and costs). I was once a telemarker who lived in Colorado but my free-heel turns were lift-served. Striding was done on trails. And the two styles never met.

My world changed for two reasons...

First I met RadNord & Company, a gang that enjoys bopping quick tele-turns as they stride the singletracks. They use today's "mt-bike of skis," a rig that is great for both striding and turning.

Then came the first time I "earned my turns"...

Earnin' Turns

Dave Jessop, a friend who lives nearby in mid-Michigan, had called a few times as I was getting ready to go to work, saying, "Hey, we just got some great powder, can you get away this morning? We have to hit it now before the sun warms it up. If you don't have gear I can find you some."

I thought he was a bit crazy with these surprise ideas. I thought I already enjoyed skiing as much as I could. I couldn't just drop work on the spur of the moment to ski up and down a bit of backwoods when during lunch I could hit a local trail and stride around in bliss. The messy deep powder in the tracks would even be skied-in by then: nice and fast. Well, Dave has had good ideas before, so maybe he was on to something. One morning when he called I said What the heck, I'll go! He told me to hurry and that I'd find suitable skis I could borrow in the back of his truck at the trailhead and to meet him and some pals at a secret spot a mile back in the woods.

I trudged in on the heavy gear. The skis didn't ski like I was used to, but I made them glide well enough. When I found the dudes at the hangout at the top of the slopes they were already grinning and covered in snow. I dropped my pack and glided with them to the brink and plunged into a world of skiing that I thought only existed in movies and on postcards of Colorado. I'd done a fair bit of telemarking and had skied powder so I relaxed into this wonderfully misplaced skiing. It was heaven! All it took was 10" of fresh snow on a base of old snow. We regrouped at the bottom, hooting and hollering then skied up the valley, then up a few switchbacks to the top again and skied some more. I noticed beers strategically placed in the snow at the top of the

Enn Poldmaa (above) hosts the hardwoods Snowflea Telefest from their B&B base near Soo, ONT. Shred, vittles, music: a full party platter. You can always tell when it's BC because of man's best friend. ...Usually not allowed in resorts of the groomed variety.

The uptrack is a thing of beauty. A time to reflect on your last run, to chat and compare notes, to rest one part of you in anticipation of using another part soon.

chugged up in unison, getting a little glide in our strides, chatting, laughing and scouting for new lines to run. They told me about how they came out in the fall and tossed aside the deadfall of the previous season to clear their lines. I knew how I liked my own autumn days taking care of local trails. I enjoyed watching the sun sparkle on the snow as we climbed. We were going slower, and it was steeper, than usual so the snow was closer and easier to marvel at. When we herringboned it was also at an easy pace since it was work enough. Still, a couple minutes and we were at the top, ready for more whoosh. Uphill and downhill were both restful and dynamic in their own ways.

climb. After an hour of exhilarating going down and exerting going up we took a break. My host pulled out of his pack a still-hot crockpot of venison stew swaddled in towels and we shared it around. Oh yeah!

As the sun swung onto us and slowed our turns a bit, I followed the gang as they set a new uptrack up a slope on the opposite side of the valley. It was still in the shade and so we kept on skiing on the still-perfect powder that they'd held in reserve.

The uphill skiing up wasn't as different from my usual skiing as the striding had been. I could use good, relaxed form. We

I was able to relax and bounce down the fall-line, thanks to the amazing new skis I was using – wider, softer and shorter than any I'd used before. I watched one of the guys ski down the trunks of fallen trees, like we were in a terrain park. I watched another do beautiful "telellel" turns through trees so close together I couldn't see between them from where I was. We put those snow-beers to good use. The dog flowed ahead of us like joyful smoke. I got home just after lunch.

The skiing was free, nearby, and with friends. I was totally won over. I'd just had a whole new dimension added to my winter world. Trail skiing goes through territory like a ribbon, while turn-skiing covers the territory like a quilt.

Such perfect snowfalls arrive downstate here only on a few special mornings. But often enough! Their scarcity amplifies the specialness.

...And that's how it happened.

Can you see why a Nordic skier might enjoy getting out in the woods for some free-spirited, free-cost freeheeling? And how the up'n'down of "earning your turns" might make sense for silent sports enthusiasts?

Any chance you'd like your gravity-sport to be FREE? And SUSTAINABLE? ...To not require the huge overhead of lift motors and enormous grooming tractors and property management and access issues?

If you're inclined to downhill turning, and you'd like to experience more of the woods, and you already enjoy uphill Nordic skiing, you're almost there.

Backcountry Culture

OK, there is a huge divide in BC culture. Actually, not a divide. There is a side that is visible and one that is invisible. The ignored side of BC actually has all the potential.

Big mountain, Rockies type, high elevation BC dominates the entire scene. It also is home to serious avalanche risk and not many people. It's about steep slopes and massive, expensive, exotic gear. It's the destination scene.

By contrast, we have the hardwoods hills of most of snow country. Full of gladed slopes and trails. Low risk. Easy access to everyone for free. ...The skiing we enjoy here is not covered or presented in the media or marketing.

My friends and I have written to the BC media pitching the glories of hardwoods BC and have never received a reply. We don't exist. ...But we could be the biggest.

I live in downstate Michigan. I wanted to get a better feel for our BC scene overall, so I called "up north" and asked my BC snow-junky pal, David Spieser, of Petoskey, what he thought about hardwoods BC. David plays hooky with his friends whenever the powder pounds. He says, "It's like an ice-skating party in the woods. There's no worry about keeping up like on a trail. Everyone does their own thing, kinda near each other, yet still exploring, dropping down to home-base after each run. Some of our favorite places don't have many trails, but they have miles of high-country slopes, like you're more used to seeing out west, like the Chandler Hills public land, where your neck gets tired from looking up so much

Scouting the mighty Chandler Hills in deciduous, hardwoods upnorth Michigan.

Big-shred BC includes plenty of striding. Here's the start of the classic uphill-downhill race at the Porkies Telefest in the UP.

and where you might not hear the sound of a motor all day. And, you know, these places are public but they are at risk of development because they're not in parks. So we'd love to see more people out there. Use it or lose it."

George Gess is a salesperson from The Outfitter in Harbor Springs, MI, host of the annual last-hurrah Telebration at Nub's Nob (usually early April). He says he's impressed by the growth in BC. "For something with no organized events and with small groups and even solo action afield, it does a good job of organizing itself. It spreads by word of mouth, from friend to friend, with everyone showing each other how it's done."

Midwest gear shops aren't always hip to the potential of their own back yards, but ever-more of them are encouraging customers to get out there and find you some slope!

In skiing, as in real estate, location is king. And the best location is where there's snow. But terrain is critical, too. If it's hilly

you can have turns, if it's mellow you have your striding. But where most of us live we can have BOTH in a lot of our outings.

John "Radnord" Rutherford is a downstate resident and also multi-time "Nordic Man" of the Midwest Telefest in the Porkies in the western U.P. The Telefest lets skiers display skills from all disciplines in one weekend of fun events in a wide variety of terrain. Youngsters are nipping at Rad's heels but every year he's gungho to make the long drive to ski the Nordic medley. He says, "The Porkies is an example of the crossroads of the Nordic world. It has it all. Groomed slopes, groomed trails, backcountry peaks and a trail linking them together, all in a big state park."

RadNord throws in tele-turns on most any trail. Trail width isn't an issue. Just stride along and when you get to a downhill throw in the jump-turns!

Bill Thompson, co-owner of Down Wind Sports in Marquette and Houghton, and host of the Midwest Telefest (February, about 150 skiers), says, "BC is 'silent sport' all the way. A few long tele runs through the trees are a massive aerobic workout. Whenever there's a big snow in this part of the state the tele skiers are off in the woods."

Enn Poldmaa and Robin MacIntyre own the Bellevue Valley B&B just north of the Soo, and they have some steep terrain. They host the truly BC, no-lifts Snowflea Telefest (Feb. 23-24, 2013, 60 people), but there are guided outings most weekends. Enn says, "New skiers come and learn and in turn become the next group's mentors. That way everyone gets a chance to be comic relief." Robin chimed in: "Gravity gets you down the hills, levity gets you up. There's so much snow that even though it's steep here, when you fall you don't get hurt. Oh, and there are a lot more women doing BC than you might think. Also, it's about good food and live music. BC is holistic. I have to say that getting the human presence into the forest is critical for curtailing the industrial presence. Glade skiers need an intact canopy to hold the snow. We've shown the high recreation value of these unique 1000 public acres and saved it from low-value pulp logging. The Laurentians are the oldest mountains in the world and it's the northern-most presence of oaks and hemlocks. It's a special place to ski!"

The Basics of BC

Why telemark? ...Because it's a way to stride and also ski big downhills using the same gear. This requires a free heel.

With a free heel you're barely attached to your skis, so to improve stability while turning the telemark turn was developed (in Telemark, Norway). By dropping low between skis that are spread out fore-and-aft and in an arced line, the skis carve, turn and behave.

To get back uphill in big mountains you use skins -- grippy fabric strips that attach to the ski base that let you march more directly up a hill then you peel 'em off and ski freely down. Modern versions are quick to use. Making gentle zigzags up such hills could take a half-hour or more. In more compact hardwood regions with uptracks that are only a few minutes duration it seems better to spend more time skiing and less time fussing so we zigzag and use

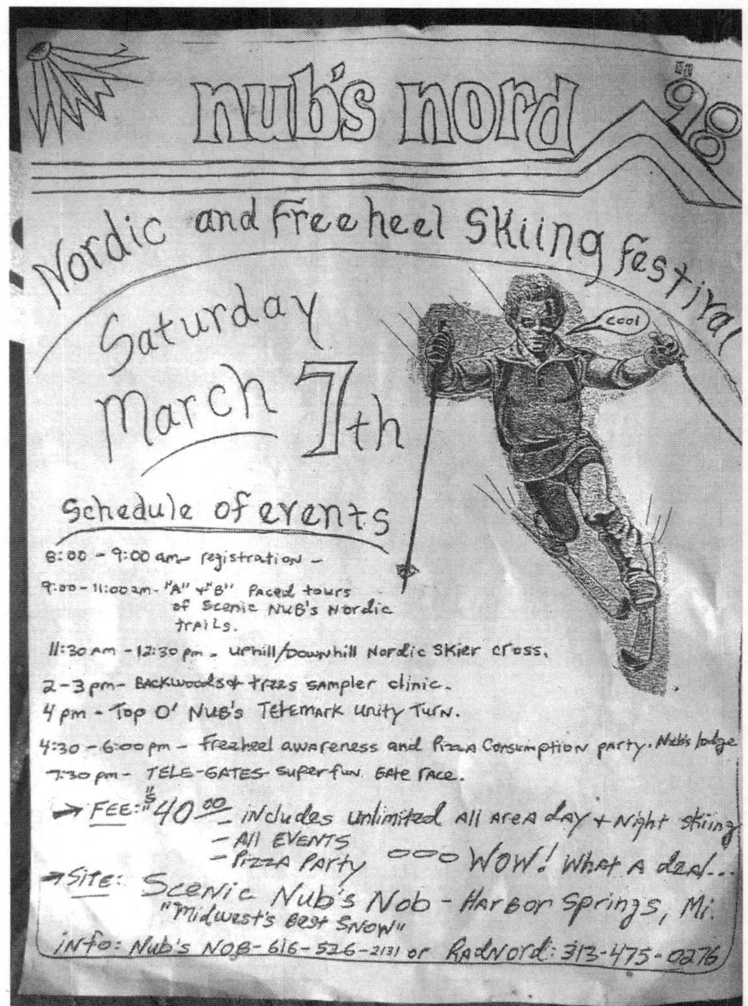

kickwax or nowax.

How to learn telemark? That's as easy as finding someone who knows! Wonderfully, today's equipment is so easy to use that you can learn to tele in a day. Getting your entre' to backcountry is just as easy, since it'll probably be the same person who shows you how to tele. Or ask at a local outdoor gear shop or google. Once you

Back in the day the Nordic experience was a combo platter. It still is...

Locally made injection molded snowshoe skis for the steep brushy watershed ravines in the UP. Thanks to the Marquette Backcountry Ski Company.

find a guide, are they your boot size? If so, it might be easier to borrow than to rent. Tele-people tend to have a "quiver," just like track skiers. A proper instructor is best, but there are a lot of helpful You-Tube videos. For your first foray go with a friend who knows.

There's bliss, freedom, camaraderie, but you need to know what you're getting into. A learning BC'er can readily transition from blue groomers to mellow, open slopes. But as soon as you drop into steeper trees, you're in double-black diamond country. Like Craig Dostie's awesome "EarnYourTurns.com" website says in its subhead: "You'll figure it out." ...Old school!

I can't not share this great tip: Nest your runs closely together. The saying is either "Mind your margins," or "Mine your margins," or both. The point is to ski all your available snow. That way a few acres can give a small group a full day of untracked powder.

In the Midwest our slopes can be mellow, so what ya do is give a push at the top to get 'em moving. (OK, I can't help but give tips.) Schuss straight until your speed is up, then as long as you, gravity and skis work together to keep a nice turning-rhythm on the way down, you're as good as gold. As they say, it's not the miles-per-hour, but the smiles. Corny, but just you see!

After you regroup at the bottom of the run set your uptrack at an angle that your nowaxers or grip wax can handle without too much herringboning. Skins aren't hardly part of the hardwoods BC game (we don't want to be fiddling with gear for our quick laps).

You're your own resort developer. You're replicating the perks of resorts in a different worldclass venue: the real snow-world, ideally near where you live.

In BC no one is telling you where and how to ski. (Also there's no ski patrol to bail you out after an injury. Use the buddy system!) You scope out the lines you like. Notice how the sun swings around. The sun makes Midwest snow heavy. Plan your day to follow the shade.

Then there's the off season. You might want to do a little autumn woodswork clearing your lines. If it's private land and you have permission, or it's yours, do as you please. If it's public, check the rules. Tossing aside deadfall is usually OK. You'll learn you don't need much space for superb turning. Do the minimum. ...Leave no trace.

Technology Breakthroughs

Recent high-tech equipment changes have given ungroomed trail-skiing a total makeover. They've done the same for "earn your turns"!

Steve Barnett, one of the main guys behind modern telemark skiing, said in an awesome interview at Dostie's site that he prefers a thrifty package probably considered too light by many: 68mm-wide, 190cm-long Madshus Glittertind skis and Salomon BC boots and bindings. That's a trail rig, some might say. Well, Barnett certainly can do a lot with it. Gear is so much better than what they used "back in the day" that Barnett says he just stays impressed, and thinks going any bigger is close to overkill. Heck, we used to use that size gear to shred black double-diamond bumps!

Before the modern era in telemark ("BMET"), BC skis were 70mm wide and an extreme ski was a 90mm repurposed downhill ski. These skis turn but require more skill, though they're easy to tour on. Today's wider, shaped, rockered skis deliver easy turning anywhere — that's not a bad wave to ride. It all depends on what you want.

BC skis now can be 125mm wide no-waxers. And they're proving fun to tour on, too! As you swim 'em along a BC trail you just can't help toss in turns as you go.

Don't short-change on adjustable or other BC-specific poles for satisfying performance both up and down. Check the reviews as some have been sketchy, but most today are light and reliable. Some favor full-length striding poles that have grips or tape added part-way down — no risk of mechanism failure — use 'em long to ski up, grab the middles for the trip down (watch the eyes).

Erich Podjaske, of the Cross Country Ski Shop in Grayling, says they're mostly a pro shop for groomed track skiing, but the BC side has taken off in the last 5 years.

"We used to have 3 models, now we have 6. They run the full range of widths from metal-edged skis that still fit in a track up to skis that are as fat as lift-served but still have nowax patterns. My saying is that BC lets you turn your favorite summer spot into a favorite all year 'round. The better skiers can do it all with a pretty thin set."

Dave Ollila, who guides the Marquette Backcountry Ski Company, maker of the only all-plastic budget ski-snowshoe, says, "With BC you don't have to obsess over skiing from lift-start to lift-close to cover an expensive lift ticket. You can grab an hour here or there on a wild slope near your house. It's a new kind of skiing which is actually the original kind. For centuries people got around on short wide skis. It's more like mt-biking or micro-adventuring. It's 'let's see what's over there.' It's rugged, great for low-snow conditions, like skiing over roots or dirt. This approach is shaking up the ski industry." (A student-run team produces these skis at Northern Michigan University.)

You can still build a cheap rig by the old routine of mounting cable bindings onto

Everyone knows what tele skis look like today: like alpine boards. They have the power, too. But just in case, here's a nice view. Fat, shaped, rockered. Let 'em fly. Looks like the downhill portion of the uphill-downhill race, sans any adjustment to the adjustable poles. ...No worries, just fan 'em out.

Ski party mayhem in the hardwoods BC at the SnowFlea Telefest near the Soo.

secondhand downhill skis (kickwax 'em for the uptracks).

The ski that sparked the recent revival of BC was the venerable Karhu Guide, the first ski that was 109mm wide with a no-wax pattern. (Now the Madshus Annum.) You could kick'n'glide 'em for a few miles then shred the trees with a grin.

A great thing about Midwest BC is you won't get avalanched. Still, consider some armor. Skiing wild means encounters with undersnow obstacles. Match pro to terrain. Trees suggest a helmet. Arcteryx makes thin knee-shields. Motocross shorts have hip padding. Some use shin-guards or thin forearm football pads.

Tele skiing in the mountains suffered an upheaval as Alpine Touring has taken over AT is lighter and more potent, if pricier. But in the mellow hardwoods where you're on the uptrack every couple minutes, and you're doing more striding, and the terrain isn't as massive, the free heel rules the roost.

Etiquette

Wild slope skiing is like beach surfing. It's like trout fishing: There's getting in the know and there's turf.

Once while we were skiing a guy told me he thought there was too much traffic on our local slope. I said, "What's too much?" He shot back: "YOU're too much!" Yeah, two's too many, sometimes.

If you're not quick and there's been a nighttime snowfall, that same guy might be out there with a headlamp, skiing it up before any of his pals wake up. It's dog eat dog, but he does the most deadfall-tossing. ...Thankfully there are a lot of hills.

I know skiers who will stand on the other side of a tree when someone is passing near. Nobody's here!

Hot tip: before you try joining a local BC scene, do your share of brush-tidying.

Users on popular trails might obliviously ski past a valley that has every inch skied after a good snowfall and yet never think there might be good slope skiing within hundreds of miles.

Trail-skiing can support thousands of users in a day, but glade skiing in the Midwest is a small-world scene.

***

So, head out with your pals and your picnic of choice. Do your own thing. Remember, earn-your-turns is what all skiing used to be. A wider ski and more supportive boot is all you need to ski and turn in the wilds. It's easy to find a set-up (or two) that lets you enjoy ALL your terrain.

Ski Party: A Backyard Biathlon

We'd had a low-snow winter. And the forecast was for 55degF in the next couple days. That would nuke what little snow we had. Then suddenly we got a dusting of fresh snow. And the yard already had a solid inch of semi-firm base....

Our local ski gang suddenly realized that this would be our last night of good snow after the work-day. So we sprang into action and texted around. Let's do a biathlon after work! We'll put out big work-lights so we can see. I jumped into gear.

Suddenly our 6pm ski-time was upon us and I realized that I should also light our bonfire! Hey, this could be more than just a little last-ditch skiing, it could be a Ski Party!

I got the fire going and dudes started showing up.

I'd borrowed large work-lights and stands from my one brother, and two more bb-guns from my other brother. All told we had 4 nice bb-guns.

We had beers and snacks, too. I turned on all our yard's holiday lights.

Five of us were the party. Everyone did some practice shooting until we were comfy with how the guns were sighted. Our targets were Gatorade pints hanging from various tree branches. If we scored a hit they made a loud and satisfying "thwack."

We wore headlamps to see where we were skiing.

We would ski a bigger lap of a few minutes of my yard trail, then shoot 3 times. If we missed we'd ski a tiny 30-second side loop then keep skiing another big loop. If we hit all 3 we could just take off on another big loop. All told we'd ski 5 big loops and shoot 4 salvos.

We took off!

We used the "track!" rule where an overtaker could holler "track" at the guy ahead and he had to pull over to let the passer by go. Of course there was cheating, so there was also passing through the woods off the trail.

Around and 'round we went! Shooting and missing and hollering. Then it was over. What a thrill! We took a snack and beer break around the fire.

Then we did it again! It was too much

fun to not keep doing it.

There's really something about skiing hard then stopping and aiming calmly then skiing hard again. It's like cyclocross: Compatible opposites blending in a satisfying mix.

Note: our biathlon was safe — enough. A bit of beer and bb-guns can mix despite any naysayers. Of course we didn't drink

enough to tell. You do it how you like depending on your own skills. We are all longtime marksmen with the reflex to muzzle control. We kept the guns pointed downrange and left them on a table, pointed downrange, after each use, and only loaded them for each shot. No neighbors or skiers anywhere in the direction of the range. These same rules apply to you, too. One set of gun safety tips to rule them all!

Last year our gang would do a night-ski each week and it often felt colder than it was. So I always try for lunch-hour ski sessions as my top priority. But this biathlon party seemed downright cozy. The loops were short. The moon was out. We were looping back around to our big bonfire every few minutes. Our colorful yard lights were always nearby. It was all around festive.

This ski party had the right mix of everything! Of course, more skiers would've been more fun.

Let's see, we had: shooting, skiing, snow, cold, night, moonlight, beer, snacks, cookies, bonfire, holiday lights, bright lights, headlights.

Oh, and the boombox! Hearing music when getting near the house was nice.

Really, biathlon is great at any time, but it's an awesome way to enhance a situation that might otherwise be short on appeal. Like, for an otherwise kind of boring or small ski loop, or if the snow isn't so hot — biathlon can spice it up.

We attempted it another time with skiing on a trail system then putting our skis away and crossing the road to a shooting range located in the park system. For me that amount of separation made it two separate outings. It took the rhythm out — and the appeal.

I also note the need to know your rifle. I missed my target my first two laps and that was discouraging. In skiing we naturally like our skis to be "just so." In biathlon we need to give just as much attention to our rifle. You have to know what it's going to do. Then you can confidently work on operator error. I was mystified by my misses and that totally ruined the experience. Then I started using another rifle, and I started hitting! What a difference that made! It really struck me how having your gun dialed in is the same as having your skis dialed in. In biathlon you need both. You quickly realize that the shooting part is not just about going through the motions. You will want it to work. Your control – or lack thereof – creates the interest.

Our next level is to figure out how to fabricate our own biathlon-slings and install them on a pellet-gun or .22. They mount to the side. But nobody wants to drill a gun-stock. Maybe we can figure out how to use zip-ties. We're thinking we could soak 2" webbing in epoxy or shoe-goo so the loops stand out stiffly like they do in official biathlons.

Biathlon shooting is usually legal on public lands that allow other shooting, like hunting. Be sure to follow your local regs. No matter what, set up your range so that the shooting has a backstop and is always directed away from other possible land-users, same as with any shooting. I like the method of hanging small plastic targets that jump around when hit. This adds the safety of never having anyone go down-range, or of having to score or re- set-up targets.

Hey, did you know that biathlon is the most popular winter sport on TV in Europe! It fills stadiums. And women's biathlon is as big as the guys. In Germany they just lowered a lady superstar in on an aerial wire for her stadium start!

Roots: Trail Work

The Foundation of Nordic

Skiing doesn't stand alone, doesn't exist by itself. You don't just buy skiing. Well, you can, but not if you want it to last. Not nowadays.

XC is grassroots.

Organized, official, commercial XC skiing today is thinner than thin.

In XC nearly everybody has to chip in on more than just the skiing for it to work.

In XC the saying is "the summer makes the skier." Well, there's even more to it. Let's find out what...

Trail Work

Skiing uses several kinds of trails. They all take work to make and to care for. Each kind needs its own care.

And here's the thing: Trailwork is good for you. Every skier should do trailwork every autumn to help get their local trails ready for the season.

Yeah, sometimes the government or a company takes care of the trails. But those probably aren't the best trails. And they sure as heck aren't singletrack. At this point singletrack skiing is a DIY scene, so if you like scenic, challenging skiing, you're going to have to contribute. That is, hook up with the local gang then get a chainsaw if you don't have one already, and keep it sharp, and find a pack for carrying it, and get ready to use it. I'm not kidding.

Shrubbery grows and trees and debris fall every year and need to be cleared before snow flies. Head out there and gitterdone. The best trailwork has a rhythm, kinda like skiing. You're out hiking along with a chainsaw or weedwacker clipped to your pack, pruners and a small shovel in your pack, a flicking stick in your hand and maybe a heavy-bladed knife on

A trail was here, and will be here again. Unless people care for trails there isn't skiing. If you ski: pay for trailwork, do it yourself, or give a lot of treats to those who do.

Superstar volunteers groom singletrack alongside the famous Au Sable River within the also-famous Mason Tract conservation area in upnorth Michigan.

of course. (One of my favorite sections of flow trail gets so many blowdowns each off-season that I can hardly see where the trail was. Keeping it clear is WORK. And I often sigh and reroute.)

In the world of bought-and-paid skiing, you might hardly think about trailwork. However, with even a little experience, skiers start to become aware of the work being done, or not done, and what they can expect in quality, and when it's good and when it's not. You'll notice when sticks haven't been picked up, or when nobody has pruned away the prickers. You'll learn how long you should wait after a snowfall before certain trails are skied-in or walked-in enough to be fun. . . . And you'll figure out what your own role should be in helping to make this happen. (A club can post a volunteer work schedule – at the trailhead, even -- to make all this easier to sort out.)

For groomed trails, whether cared for by volunteers or staff, you might come to know who does what kind of quality of work and when. You'll learn about how long to wait to ski after the groomer goes through.

In the biggest, ungroomed world of "just plain skiing anywhere there's snow" trailwork by everyone who skis is an essential part of each pre-season.

In the autumn all around the XC ski world, skiers head out to the forests and start getting things ready for winter. Trees have fallen since the last snows of spring. Obstacles that haven't been a bother for biking, hiking or running might want to be altered for skiing. Certain parts of properties might be set aside for skiing and un-

one hip and a folding saw on the other.

You stride along at a good clip getting everything off your trail that might bother a ski come snowfall. Flick off all the little sticks, kick aside the stones. Move logs, saw trees. Prune away the eye-pokers that have grown in from the summer. Use the manual or motor weedwacker to knock back the prickers and wild roses that have grown in. Keep it moving and you'll work up a sweat. You might get a mile done in an afternoon, depending on everything, used the rest of the year. Skiing basically leaves no trace and the forest doesn't care that a certain route through it is great for skiing so it might need to be sorted out again before it's easy to use, or else the ski trail has to go some other way, which can be easy enough to make happen.

Last I read there are 350 official Nordic areas in North America. Maybe a hundred of these are sizable.

Snowmobile trails sometimes have sizable license funding and their own groomers. They can be good for skiing, especially ski skating, but beware of traffic and avoid prime times for machines, like weekends.

Places to Earn Your Turns…

For downhill skiing where it's cold and gets a lot of snow and is at altitude and has grooming or snowmaking you can have open downhill slopes exposed to the sun that can still be made to hold snow. These trails are wide swaths that run down the fall-lines of slopes – ski runs of various ratings.

For downhill skiing if you want a slope to hold snow you want it to be north facing and forested. You clear out the undergrowth but leave the trees to shade the snow so it lasts.

For earn-your-turns skiing such slopes can be anywhere. The length of their pitches is limited by the geography of the region as well as by how much time the skiers care to spend hiking back up the up-tracks to ski again. For any region, 100 yards is a nice pitch. This size can clearly be found in typical hard-

woods hills.

What you do is find a chunk of land with a slope that you have access to and in the fall kick aside enough deadfall to clear a safe way down through the trees once the ground freezes and enough snow flies. It also helps to scout out a pleasant uptrack route where you can regain the top of your slope conveniently – some log moving might be required for this as well. Depending on the rules of your property you might have as much liberty for slope preparation as a hunter would have when preparing a blind or treestand, that is, it might be OK to remove some saplings. Or you might get a firewood permit for cutting deadfall. Know your trees, shrubs and plants of local value and don't change anything improperly.

Ideal slope for glade-tidying starts at a location with minimal brush and deadfall. An afternoon of tossing logs can deliver days of powder turns in the BC! (This northern Michigan valley has already been winding uphill steeply for a half-mile.)

Roots: Training — Get Ready!

Skiers are made in the summer.

...And don't you forget it! For casual trail purposes, though, it's OK if they're made in the fall.

General XC ski-type fitness is easy to learn about online or in many books. So I won't bother with that. Instead I'll give you a taste of the special fun we want to have when getting ready for an everyday sort of Nordic reality.

Even if you're a mellow skier you really need to get ready for skiing each fall. It's part of the reality of climate change. You want to be sure you can enjoy all the snow you get. You might be getting less snow each year than you'd like, but that's no reason not to ski the heck out of what you do get. And there's only one way to do that: be prepared. Hit it when it starts and don't look back. Don't get tired! For low-snow skiing you don't want to be caught needing to ski yourself into shape. You'll need to take a break and conditions will just be sitting there, gorgeous. Or by the time you're able to have big fun it'll melt out from under you. Don't let either bad thing happen!

What are the basics? Skiing requires coiled leaping of the whole body. So you want all-body fitness. You want cardio endurance fitness over a full range of motion. You're gonna want to spend an hour or two playing around out there. At least a half hour. Some amount of time where you can settle in and enjoy ski handling and rhythm.

Since skiing is a weight-bearing sport that rewards uphill glide you want to be friends with gravity. You're gonna want to be as skinny as you can be. Thankfully, you'll save money because you'll eat less.

Until this stuff is ingrained into your life-style you need a gang that likes to meet up 2 or 3 times weekly.

It's not hard! The memory of skiing last season plus the brisk tang in the air in autumn that signals the changing of the seasons will get you psyched. You'll be out there during the most glorious days of color time! It's nature's spectacular. Don't miss any of it! Share it!

And you'll still be gung-ho while the clueless drones are feeling low in the grey, rainy gloom after the leaves are down but before the snow flies.

Pulling stout Thera-Band elastic tubing is awesome for poling fitness. I use the strongest grade. I tie loops in a tree to imitate poling. I also anchor a loop down low to train pole-recovery. I also work core, plus I do shoulders for paddlesports.

25 years of yardwork. Chuck Norris slider at the back is the latest addition: it's awesome. Replicates the classic slider-board perfectly. I kneel on it and do double-poling with ab firing. (Further back is my lifesaving 3'x15' Hillbilly Infinity pool for defeating summer humidity.)

Here's the big twist of XC: it uses the most energy of anything. So you need to build up your ability to tolerate the energy load. If you just play around like usual, that won't be enough. You really should train up in the fall to be able to put out more work than you ever would usually. Only then will you be ready for the increased workload of daily ski-play.

Any fitness is great, but really you need to be extra-fit. If you hit that first snow with typical fitness you'll be sore and tired in a few days.

XC uses upper and lower body and you're going up hills. You need to build up to handling that!

What's more, skate-skiing uses more muscle (less aerobics) and so it puts a bigger load on the body than classic does.

If by the time fall rolls around you're comfy with a few hours of biking, a couple hours of canoeing, or an hour of running, then you're ready for a daily half hour of vigorous XC skiing in cold conditions. Something like that. In short: XC-plus-cold isn't "harder," it just puts a bigger load on you than other activities.

Seeing Stars

XC skiing is special in that you can easily *go under* at most any point in an outing if you hit it hard enough. If you go hard enough, often enough you're gonna see stars. And pretty soon moving your arms will feel like stirring mud. You'll find yourself saying "I'm just going to pull over here for a bit and stop and try to remember how to use words again."

Another crazy thing is that because of the low-impact and the soft landings, once you're fit you can go so hard you see stars over and over again.

Stars aren't nearly as bad as a bonk, though. That's where you use up all your glycogen stores while not being ready to switch to a lower output fat burn. That is truly a terrible time for low energy drooling gibberish. An outing is basically shot then. Good luck limping home. (If you're going out for more than a couple hours, bring food and eat it.)

When people are new to skiing it might be hard for them to realize how easy it is to go too hard. When they start going faster maybe they start floundering or crash before they can actually get breathing heavily. This is why, if fitness is a goal, you need to master the basics of stable skiing so you'll have a solid enough platform from which to kick out the jams.

Load Limit

Since we can easily go so hard in XC, RECOVERY is key to building up. In low snow eras we are easily tempted to ski hard every day there's snow! But if we want to ski more or faster during a winter we have to go easy sometimes. Ironically, our fickle weather warm-ups and spells of no-snow can help with this. We ski like crazy when we have snow then rest when it melts, re-energizing for the next good snowfall. (It is kind of fun, actually, though not mentioned in any ski media I've ever seen.)

You'll want to do some kind of trail running most autumn days. Bring poles along to get the arms in on it. Throw in sections of trail-bounding where you imitate skiing. And add a few uphills where you can really imitate skiing.

If you want to do longer ski outings, be sure to do dryland outings of comparable lengths a few times each fall. If your ski outings will include a loaded pack, be sure to carry one in the fall also. Of course, we're better able to do those longer autumn outings if we've also been doing them in the summer and spring. It's far easier maintaining fitness than it is acquiring it!

Spending active time outdoors is really how we should be living year-round!

Basically, what you build up to in the fall is what you'll be able to do in skiing.

Tricks of the Trade

If you want to learn real skiing and expand your skills beyond ski-walking, a few dryland outings with poles and some dryland imitation of skating will do wonders for TEACHING. The casual touring stride is fine, as is just kind of getting around in skate-skiing, but both of these are characterized by LATE POLING. This is mostly a problem on uphills. Dryland, by contrast, is simple and you time your poling with your leg-action to do it. Problem solved. That habit will carry over easily to the snow.

It's also traditional to do pulling exercises to imitate ski poling. Design your versions of these for both single-poling and double-poling. A common method is to tie bike inner tubes up in a tree or anything else above head-height. Then you stand back and pull on them like you're skiing and double-poling. You can also buy the awesome product called Thera-Band Resistance Tubing. The strongest grade is Silver. Rainwater runs off of it better than it does off of inner-tubes. I like doing arm-

Enjoying the charms of the Chuck Norris "Total Gym" garage sale special. I do reps a couple times a week year-round. Combined with everything else, it works. I never get overly over-tired once skiing commences. I keep the training casual so it's never boring, stressful or ineffective. I keep it fresh so I keep doing it. Daily all-body action is awesome, invigorating R&R!

The awesome CAT Skis are true offroad rollerskis. They don't care where you use 'em. Big training effect plus they actually teach proper kicking and penalize you when you get sloppy.

pulls year-round with mine, but I pick up the frequency and intensity in the autumn. Usually, I pull on bands only for a minute or two. (I never do an exercise in a way that's vexing or disinclines me to it.) ...I've been pulling on elastics tied up above head-height for, um, 30 years.

You can also devise an inclined sliding board for belly or kneeling arm-work. There are online plans. The Chuck Norris fitness machine uses the same concept. (OK, it's also the Christie Brinkley Total Gym, but I'll stick with Chuck since he controls the weather and so is cool.) This is a kind of armwork that's like elastic bands but perhaps works the abs more. It's fun as variety. ...And I find that these machines are available in thrift-shops or on Craigslist everywhere for $20. I've left mine outside in all weather for years. I sometimes spray the tracks with lube.

Dips are also a mainstay exercise for

skiers, working the triceps, shoulders and upper back.

Here's something: I've read that the quantity of dips, push-ups, pull-ups and box-jumps done in a short time are together the most significant predictors of ski success. (Google the Canadian Strength Test.)

Other great all-round fitness activities in the fall are biking, cyclocross and paddling. ...And the awesome stars of yardwork and rural living: leaf-raking, firewood-splitting and tree chopping.

How to imitate hills if you live where there aren't many? Hillwork gives you power no matter what kind of skiing you'll do, even for flat-land.

If you don't have hills, add resistance. Gunde Svan in the early 80's was seen running forest trails pulling a log tethered behind him. Nowadays quite a few wackos boost their power by running or rollerskiing while pulling a small car tire attached to them with a bungie and waist-strap (or to a rucksack). ...It turns every outing into a bit of an uphill! People also just carry weight in a ruck while they train, or wear a weight-vest.

Then there's snow-removal! Shoveling snow can be a frustrating rival to skiing when you come home from work after a good snowfall and you would like to go ski. Well, you have to bite the bullet and fit it all in! Your fall training will really come in now. You'll need to do snowblowing or shoveling and then maybe some trail-breaking before you can ski. Or do what you can to farm it all out! Don't overdo it early in the winter.

Rollerskiing

Don't neglect specificity. You're going to be skiing for the rest of your life. It's not going to let you go. So you might as well buy rollerskis: for skating, for striding, and Cat Skis. If you use each of these at least a few times every autumn you'll be awesomely ready when the snow flies. They last longer than skis so you can think of their cost as amortized over 10-20 years – which makes them pretty thrifty!

Rollerskis are the best and most efficient way to train for skiing. Because they are skiing. So if you're short on time, do that for best results. With smooth pavement and sharp poles they can be pleasant.

If you don't want rollerskis at least get inline skates and use ski poles.

You need to identify a place to rollerski that is safe and smooth. Rollerskis are notorious they are all somewhat sketchy, even the ones with brakes. Some rollerskis are more tolerant of debris than others. I've long used V2 Aero 125's with inflatable tires. They're the only type I can tolerate on my main route which is chipsealed.

People often use a helmet and pads for rollerblading: even smarter for rollerskiing.

It's best to limit it to very moderate terrain. There's a lot of rollerskiing on YouTube, but remember most of it involves coached teams, special venues, and vehicles to bring skiers downhill.

The only reason to do such a risky activity is that it's so darn effective for getting ready to ski.

Classic rollerskis are difficult to stride with. You must make yourself ski correctly. The skis will let you cheat if you don't.

C.A.T. Skis

There is a kind of classic rollerski that actually HELPS your technique. It teaches you to ski better. For some reason it's not popular among any elites but it should be. Maybe it's because "serious" classic skiing today doesn't actually involve all that much skiing: Classic racing is dominated by double-poling. Boring! It's a problem that could be solved by hillier courses but there are limits to that in the rules. It is most easily remedied by Trail Skiing. Those who ski singletrack hiking and biking trails spend nearly all their time enjoying the glories of striding.

This alternative classic rollerski is the CAT Ski: the Classic All Terrain Ski. Created by Dale Niggemann, engineer. It's not a typical rollerski. It's hard to explain but it works. It's the only truly offroad rollerski. It is safe -- which is huge! It is stable and works on grass, leaves, dirt, pavement, slush. (Order at Catskier.com.)

It's a rule in skiing that when you're gliding you're slowing. So it's an error to "try" to glide. Glide is a result of conditions, power, and tempo. If you try to glide on CAT Skis you will run into the end of them and hear a loud "clack" and might stumble. So kick them instead. You cannot overkick the CAT Ski. And kicking is what you want to learn. These devices teach good skiing!

Since you use them only when striding you might think that you can't use them to train double-poling, but you can, and even use them to train for skating. See YouTube for info.

I use CAT Skis in the fall for short sessions, mostly for variety. I also use them

Stretch and warm-up before any outing…

in bad weather or when I don't want to go out on a road. Like every part of my training, I use them in a way that keeps me interested.

Just Get Outside and Do Stuff!

"Unlimited: A Year in Oxygen-fed Sport" was a feature-length DVD film that revealed the Nordic way of life. It was presented as a year in outdoor sports through the seasons. No one sport was meant to be emphasized, but the interesting thing is that Nordic skiers are the people who seem most likely to be doing all these things, doing the year-round seasonal variety of playing outside.

I've always enjoyed doing all sorts of outdoor activities, but as I get older I find it easier to keep doing them without doing anything that seems extra. I exercise weekly with enough variety so I can do any of it in my casual way – and have a lot of fun with all of it. At this point I can haul off and ski, bike, paddle, hike or chop, rake or work all day without it being a problem

and without any special "getting ready" needed. Of course, I'm always doing a little something or another whose effect is keeping me ready for any of it. I don't get all that sore after new things, either. …One of the perks of getting older with a diverse fresh-air lifestyle.

Getting Serious

A quirky datapoint that Coach Antonina Anikin used to teach us and her Russian Olympic athletes is that humans have 100,000 heartbeats a day to work with. Do the math. Use them as you like. But if you work out any more than that you'll overtrain.

If you want to ski faster, my best tip is to ski with faster people. (This is true for any sport.) Mooch along with them and hang on to them as long as you can. They may well be doing more than you can, so take shortcuts, skip a lap. Or you can do one of your hard days when they're going easy.

Especially if you ever get a chance to ski and hang out with Europeans, do it! They have a different, more inclusive ski culture than we can imagine even at our upper levels. They're fun! They ski so close together. Tip to tail for classic and overlapped in skating. And they horse around. (I got to hang out with some top NCAA Euro's for a week once. They kept building ski jumps in the middle of ski outings. Fun!) They are good at mixing life with sport because their lives ARE sport in an immersive way. They just do it. The way we do it might not be so sociable. Now, the world has become globalized and culture is shared more today, so it might be that some US scenes have acquired Scandi stylepoints.

Downsides of Serious

Several factors other than skill determine sports results when you really step up your game. Talent and interest aren't enough. Other genetics come in. You have to withstand the required workload without injury, sickness, fatigue or malaise. Then, in the US, you'll need a lot of money. It's like this for all our sports with lower corporate sponsorship.

For some it's worth it. So we give our heroes the props both for what they do and what they sacrifice.

Then there's plateauing. After doing outdoor things for a few years you tend to not get better. This can be deflating if you've gotten hooked on the improving bug. The dread beasts "patience" and "acceptance" rear their heads: can you accept you as you are, rather than the you who was "always moving up"?

I have to issue another caution: people in sport can consider a friend or peer who finishes behind them as being lesser in more ways than genetics or hours trained. Race results affecting social status is a thing. Careful!

Health . . .

XC skiers are at the biggest risk of catching colds of anyone! But if you act quick, you can prevent or reduce them. Everyone needs to learn their own way of handling a cold! ...Hit the water bigtime, vitamin C megadoses, zinc tablets, Zicam nasal swabs: anything and everything. ...And go easy that day, but don't just lay around. Get out for light fresh air activity.

When we do start doing outdoor sports as a year-round lifestyle it's good to be aware of range of motion issues. XC (and all its friends) works the body in a fairly limited range of motion. This raises the risk of repetitive motion injury, and weakness outside of the range. Act to reduce this! Yes, it means doing even more! Mix it up.

Singletrack and telemark expand the range of XC motion. (Mt-biking expands cycling. Rolling expands paddling.) Extra calisthenics for diverse motions is smart.

Make sure your joints are strong against common wipe-outs. When people wipe out they often stop a fall with outstretched arms which stresses the shoulders -- so stretch and exercise in a wide range to beef them up. Do bone-stimulating shock exercises -- like log-chopping!

You might benefit from sauna. Some prefer hot tubs. Massage -- manual and with rollers and tools. Now that I'm a tough old buzzard I find I don't need these as much. They're nice! But I used to need them to survive. (Poor young people.)

Lastly, old fart hammerheads are running into A-Fib by the score: I guess a lifetime of hammering for the thrill is hard on a body. Seems as good a reason as any to value moderation and develop every aspect of convivial recreation rather than focusing on race results or the endorphin training high. Too bad sense and civilization don't have as much influence as a scary chest feeling. Let's grow up!

Roots: Social Work — Support Your Sport

Everyone should be part of a local club or group and make sure you're volunteering or working events as a key part of your mix. Like if you ski 10 events a season, definitely volunteer at least one. If you don't have a local club, start one. Then announce your existence to everyone who might be interested.

By club I mean any kind of group. Maybe people don't like groups these days. So use some other kind of better, more effective social set-up. Just remember to pay it forward. If everybody doing it on their own seems best, fine. If synergy and teamwork might get more done, make a plan. Build, care for, clear, some trail. Teach people how to ski. Loan gear. . . . Especially to kids, teens, and 20-somethings.

Roberts Rules is still the standard for organizational set-ups. And, guess what, if you use these basics, and the standard Board Bylaws format, you can get grants. If you become a 501c3 you can get even more. This could be a way to replace some of our lost XC infrastructure.

Make sure your club is reaching out to kids. The easiest way to do this is through Scouting, but schools are an option, too.

Young people can be age-ist, but we need to do our part to reach out and not give them an excuse to shun us if we happen to be wrinkled.

(I remember when I started ski racing and Butch Stockton was winning everything every year. He was in his 40's. He was also winning everything in the summer in pro canoe racing. I was doing my best to close in on him. I remember thinking someday maybe I can be as fast and tough and wrinkled as him! That's hilarious now to think of wrinkles as cool and a sign of speed.)

Biking might contain yet another object lesson for skiing. Organized century rides seem to be aging while "gravel grinders" and casual S24O's ("sub 24-hour overnights") are booming. They are comprised

A meeting of the SEMIFUHOs in their conference room. Really, could be a legit meeting! (Southeast Michigan Funhogs.)

mostly of millennials. We have to find the kind of skiing that offers a style that younger people can enjoy. Or we have to hope they create it themselves as they have done with cycling.

We should also try to teach others to ski and let the public know that your club members are available to help. We should each work on our own way of teaching, a way that we verify works for us. Perhaps biking has had an easier go of revival because it's less of a taught activity and the learning curve is shorter.

Our clubs, or social groups, should also do what they can to replace the hundreds of disappeared rental and family trade-in programs. Hand me down ski gear can be made available. Thrifts can be gleaned.

Our sport should be accessible to those of lower income and to honestly poor college students. This mostly means frequent recreational outings and events without entry fees. Carpooling. Fundraising. Sharing of floor space at lodging. Trail skiing that reduces the influence that expensive fragile skis and expensive fluorocarbon wax have on our level of fun. Less of an emphasis on racing and more on picnicking.

We need to reach out to other genders and ethnicities. Winter happens to everyone in snow country, so everyone should be exposed to what it means to break through to healthy fun in the snow. Socializing and building bonds and friendships are the name of the game.

Organizations of some flavor are key to making this happen. It doesn't happen by itself. It will disappear if we don't act.

From what we see in the general culture, it appears that traditional social groups are passe'. ...Except you better associate with one or get one organized for XC in your area if you want to have fun or save the children.

Build a website, add a Facebook group, a forum, a Page, create an email list. Whatever it takes.

Clubs are also great for PR, networking and accountability. XC and Outdoor clubs are also good for keeping an eye on forests, parkland and developers.

Ski Party: A Low Snow Raid

The Potto Raid on the Potawatomi Trail in Pinckney, Michigan, was once again a success.

About 20 showed up to attempt the 18-mile technical singletrack trail or portions of it. ...Or just the party afterward!

It's a self-supported outing and we expect to take 3 to 4 hours to finish. That's a long time for "just" 18 miles, but the Poto is hillier and trickier than most trails.

Now, it's true that when riding it in summer it's very hard to imagine SKIING such a technical trail! It seems impossible! Yet every winter, there we are, having so much ski fun there, whether the snow is thick or thin. When it's deep it's a superb electra-glide. But even when it's thin it's tasty.

It's named the "Potto" after the spelling used for early 1980's bike events held on the trail before it was signed, before anyone knew the right spelling, and before it became a regionally famous MTB trail. Nowadays it's usually spelled Poto.

But our host RadNord has been running events here since back in the day and he likes his old spelling.

We call it a Raid because it sounds cool and it's more like a gentleman's event run in stages than a race per se. We've read of Raids in European smallboat events that have race portions throughout a larger overall event, not just non-stop races. They're meant to encourage partying as well as skill. Raid is also a ski-mountaineering term for a big, technical ski challenge. We combine the concepts. I guess it's also like an MTB Enduro.

Speaking of combining things: our downstate XC BC Series is developing connections to local businesses who like being part of fresh air culture! Lansing's Midtown Brewing Company sponsored our Raid apres' ski party. Arbor Brewing and Brewery Becker have joined for other events! Skiing is social and we welcome – and reward – anyone who likes fun and a challenge! Thirst is a natural part of this. It's great that our local microbreweries support fresh air fun. ...And guess what, there's

little happening in the winter around here for PR so XC is attractive to sponsors!

For our Raid stages set-up, we have a neutral first half hour for chatting, photos, and for people to get familiar with the conditions of the day and the style of the trail if they haven't skied it much. Then we have subsequent stages highlighting Downhill, Flats, and an Uphill Finale, with snack stops and partial regroupings between each.

It's highly recommended to get to know what skiing the Poto is like before the Raid. Go out beforehand on your own and try some of the signature hills, both up and down. At first even though I'm an expert skier I practiced the downhills a half at a time until I could do them calmly from top to bottom. If a portion gave me trouble, I'd go back to the sticky part and do it over. Many good skiers take off their skis and walk some downhills. Or they carefully sidestep an upper portion to avoid building up too much speed. It's hard to snowplow and scrub speed on a rocky, steeply dropping gullied-out downhill. The Poto has caused loss of blood, injuries and broken gear. Respect it!

There are a few tricks for handling gullied drops. One is to drag a ski or both skis in deeper snow on the sideslopes. Another is to glide with an outer ski high up the side of a gully and the inner ski angled, plowing and scrubbing speed. Sometimes both skis need to drag but you can't do a snowplow in a gully so you do more of a parallel plow, with both tips angled down the hill but off to the same side.

The Poto is more technical than any groomed ski trail. It's more of a trials experience. Ski stepping and ski placement in particular split-seconds are occasionally critical. Speed scrubbing is done creatively. There's also little room for herringboning up an eroded, rooty, rocky climb. The sidestepping "skidaddle" is the move of choice, as is carefully stepping up and past obstacles while staying relaxed. Pole plants and timing take on new meaning.

A low-snow Raid sees many using some protection, depending: helmet, knee-pads, hip pads, forearm pads.

After a half hour we take a break, strip clothes, eat a bit, then faster skiers step it up and start to get into their rhythm.

That's when the biggest technical downhills are encountered. The leader after this stage is declared to be the downhill champ. We take another break at the halfway. Now skiers show up in clusters for a rest and snack. After this the power stage kicks in. Also, some take a shortcut.

Yet another custom trick of this event is the patented method for crossing high-arched wooden bridges with siderails. Can't ski or herringbone them so we take off poles and grab one side of the fence and do a half-sided herringbone up.

After an hour of crossing bridges and meadows, climbing and descending ridges, we come to the last rest stop on a boardwalk overlooking an expanse of marsh. Now only a very few will gather for the final bites of pizza and rewaxing. The last stage has an extended, twisting, technical uphill nicknamed Alp de Wheeze plus a few more technical downhills.

Good luck to everyone on keeping it together for the whole trail!

This year was warm and slushy with a wet half-inch of clear, watery snow substance over top of a nice half-inch of clear icy base. Admiring the glowing autumn leaves showing through the translucent snow added a beauty to the experience.

Nowax skis were the tools of choice. I used old full-length sandpaper-base zero-

type skis that didn't buzz like everybody else's fishscales. Mine had better glide, too, which I was able to milk, so I gradually inched off of the front — to the consternation of stronger, faster youngsters on new midlengths.

Ski choice for the Raid never involves high tech prep. It's more big picture. Those concerned about safety sometimes opt for metal edges. Sometimes conditions are good enough that some are tempted to use race skis, though it hasn't been tried yet. Usually something in between is the answer. But what? Full-length skis glide better but are hard to handle on the tricky climbs and descents. Midlengths handle ice and turns best. Your skill level gives the answer. Good snow hints at waxables but 3-4 hrs of skiing around here always means changing conditions and rewaxing. Don't do it too often! Raids have been lost due to just one rewax stop too many. I like Grip Tape when we have real snow but if it's thin this is unwise: it rubs off on exposed roots. The best solution is: use what works for you!

The lead group was jumpy, with Ben going off the front between early stages. ("Is he going to wait up? What if he doesn't?") And then Jen -- our fast gal -- cruised away into the overall lead. Both moves served to provoke the pace in the early stages before the halfway. We were still trying to keep a "chatting pace" going by mutual consent but Jen was gaining "diesel time." ..."If she gets too many minutes on us, it's game over, boys."

After a half hour of this we took another break. Ben was there waiting. But Jen wasn't! After that rest I started stringing moves together rather than pausing at each uphill and downhill. I eventually saw Jen in the distance.

This year, I had thankfully figured out my knee problem (wear a brace) and my foot-nerve problem (pad the undertoe with foam) and so my body stayed together.

(Last year my body failed me. I was in the lead at the ¾ point when I unraveled. I was fit! I was hammering! But then a knee stopped working. Then a foot felt like it caught on fire. So I just stopped and stood there. . . . While several sweaty rascals trounced past me, laughing. What happens after the hammer drops isn't pretty.)

I waited for a few skiers close behind at the halfway snackstop. But after that the hammer dropped. I inched off the front again but suddenly had clothing malfunctions. A shirt fell out from under my fannypack lashings. Only hollering alerted me. So I waited for Dan to bring it up. My cinch-straps keep losing gear! I should spray them with grippy stuff. Then my suspenders fell off! I tied them around my shoulders as quick as I could. I lost a minute and Stan was gone off the front.

I was with Dan and Gary and they speculated that it might now all be over. They were chatting and I thought we could be going hard enough to make talking include more panting. So my good-gliding skis took me back on my way again and I gradually saw Stan then reeled him in.

Everyone tries to ski within themselves at this point, an hour from the finish, but here's where seeing someone with a bit more glide can be demoralizing even if you only lose a few seconds. Gary did it to me last year. This year I inched away from Stan after I caught him.

It was wet and slushy, and getting stickier, and I had to doublepole the downhills, but I also encountered some shadier firm areas that glided OK. I figured that Stan was out-horsepowering me in the sticky stuff so I kept trying to milk everywhere

else. I kept the pressure up into, on, and over all climbs. No missteps. Even so, I fell and stumbled a couple times. It's a tricky trail! Each time I biffed I knew the gap had narrowed. It's like cyclocross where each move adds up and where each mistake costs a couple seconds that are hard to undo.

I encountered Bernie who had taken the halfway shortcut. He asked "How many are ahead?" I said None!

We were in a big bowl area of forest and I thought to keep an ear peeled for when I heard Bernie's resonant voice again. Sure enough, after less than a minute I heard him hollering back there. He must be talking to Stan! There were still a dozen tricky climbs and technical descents to come. Anything could happen!

I tried to ski as if Stan was just in front of me. I thought "It's a half hour remaining. Treat it like a short cyclocross race!"

When bad things happen to good skis. ...Dan still finished!

YO FREE HEELED SKIER FREAKS AND OUTLAWS:

WHEN: Sunday January 7, 2018 10:00 am (also ski the Stinch Lopett 1/21/18, Fire n Ice 2/3/18, Mason tract 2/24/18 and Jordan Jam 3/3/1. All 5 make up the MI back country series.)

WHERE: On the world famous POTTO trail. Silver Lake main lot.

WTF: A 17+ MILE BACK COUNTRY SKI RACE.

WHY: Need to ask, don't bother showing up.

WHO: Open to all who dare. Any, and all, Nordic Freaks welcome.

Better wear knee pads and duct tape your heels.

PRIZES:

1ST PLACE: CHEESEY GOLD MEDAL, lack of respect and ridiculing from your peers.

2nd PLACE: LONELINESS AND DESPAIR. Various cool shwag for odd categories as well. Might be some FREE BEER.

Don't miss this opportunity to really mess up your skis, blister the piss out of your heels and maybe, just maybe, bash your knee on a rock.

Contact RadNord at (734) 417-4227 for more info and to register. GO FOR THE GOLD or

stay home and knit with all the other sad sacks.

Really, I just tried to keep moving and to not screw up or blow up.

At the finish I had a few minutes on Stan who had a few on Dan. Those youngsters are closing in! Then came Gary, Rad and Ben.

Ben lost his bottle of Gatorade somewhere and was standing along the trail bonking at an hour to go when Rad passed him. He asked Ben how he was doing. Ben said "Bad. No food or water." Rad put the hammer down. …That's what he did to me last year!

Over the next half hour Jen and all the rest came in. Everyone was beaming from having "cleaned" yet another tricky Poto. …No blood! Actually, some of them might not even have fallen.

Rad works for Jiffy Mix and sponsored many muffin-mix door prizes and the deluxe podium sixpacks at the parking lot party. (A freshly released Bell's Hopslam six for the winner!) Some years we have a bonfire.

I wrung out my socks, changed footwear and relaxed. *Ahhh!!* Everyone changed into warm clothes, then we cranked up the car stereo, and rehashed the action. Everyone was impressed by how good the conditions were for being so bad!

The hardwood ridges and lake views of the Poto are unmatched. And the flow of the trail is unrivaled for skiing satisfaction. A few weeks later I went up north and skied a top-shelf groomed trail system. The lack of flow or challenge was noticeable. I missed our technical downstate action. I guess I'm just hooked on cyclocross-type skiing! …Stringing together each piece of footwork determines the flow.

It's always fascinating to all those who ski the Poto, all of whom also love to mt-bike it in the summer, how none of the groomed-course type Nordic skiers will even try the Poto. "Serious" skiers don't seem willing to try diverse skiing in general. We've had one racer-type do the Raid in 10 years. He seemed to have a great time, but he came from across the state and now has little kids. Really, the Poto welcomes and rewards all hardcore skiers!

Skilz: How to XC Ski for Normal People

Here's where I show you how to ski. I note that I include several techniques not taught elsewhere that are fun and useful for regular people to learn everyday skiing. Get ready!

I have YouTube videos at my Outyourbackdoor channel that teach skiing better than text can. But best of all would be a class in person with someone who will treat you right.

Ski lessons used to be a thing. Ski pros were cool. In XC classes were everywhere in Community Rec programming, but both low-snow and social trends have faded this scene. Taking classes is fun! We're missing out. Let's see if we can build it up again and make it a good time.

I've been studying and sharing XC skiing in all its forms for decades -- playing-with, comparing notes, discussing, and teaching.

My goal here is the most direct way to get you into the sweet-spot for fun. No excess. I even like skipping words when I can in actual classes.

Hey, if you live in mid-Michigan and want a lesson, let me know! I do solo sessions for $40. An hour will do ya. Groups are $20 a head. ... Jeff@outyourbackdoor. com.

This isn't really a how-to book. The photos in particular aren't exhaustive. Mostly I use ones that show things other books don't.

I'm not PSIA certified. I suppose mostly it's folks associated with resorts who have that card. They teach a race-based style, anyway. I start from everyday life and let folks add race techniques as is useful.

In real life I do a bit of substitute teaching. So I have my ways, at the same time, I don't have a teaching degree. And in a way I'm subbing here! I wrote this book because the ski industry has skipped out of considering the needs of average people who want to ski in their neighborhood park. I'm filling in. (I also wrote it because it's the kind of book I like to read!)

I also include info that will help jaded experts get a fresh take on their sport and widen their skill-range. Check it and see!

This info should be helpful, but you should get personal instruction from a pro. Even a skier friend who is also a good observer and explainer of what you need can be helpful. (Not all skiers can teach!) But there's no replacing a class!

Of the books in print Steve Hindman's "Cross Country Skiing" is by far the best. It's concise and pro, even though, per usual, it is inclined to race technique.

My method is designed to deliver the 3 basic virtues of all snowsport -- *glide, *rhythm, *pay-off -- without excess. At the same time, there are 3 main learning styles: hearing, seeing, doing. In a class I would be observing you to see how you learn. Here I'll come at concepts from various directions while still being direct. (Ha!)

This isn't lowest-common-denominator. We're not just walking here. It's time to dance!

Here's what you need to do to XC ski: *Be in the "ready position" at all times! *Use your arms normally! *Plant your foot -- grip gives all glide.

All failures in XC involve not doing the above three things.

All success requires going back and forth on flat ground learning to do these three things.

Then we need you to do these same three things GOING UP HILL. (You won't be able to do it unless you do the three things.)

All my teaching info that follows is designed toward those 3 things.

Now, maybe you're already out there having fun on skis. It's easy to go out and get by just cruising along. Then for the uphills you just trot and all is good. You don't really need a lesson to do basic "ski shuffling" or rumpushing around. But if you want to savor gliding UP the hills, and be confident jamming down the hills and around the bends, you'll need a class. You can also have a beneficial hour learning my method here and on-screen.

YouTube videos can be a very good source of info. I've made a dozen of them with over 300k combined views. I think people like mine because I'm the only one who shows casual skiing, like it really is for most people, without a technical, analytical racing perspective. They're primitive, but I guess they work. You won't find other videos on trail skiing. For learning race methods, there are dozens of videos, some with top production values, especially if you like vector arrows overlaid comparing the angles of various rapidly moving body parts.

On my OutYourBackdoor channel I also link to several of the professional race-type ones that stand out to me for having concepts anyone could use.

Caution! Consider what you're told by any kind of instruction in light of it working for you. At the same time, without help you will violate basic principles and you will flounder and suffer and make wrong adaptations just to kind of get around. Your kludges might work pretty good, but you would be better off if you back up and sort out the basics.

Also, the people who know the "right" way tend think casual skiers, no matter how dialed in they are, are "doing it wrong." So there's that.

We can have so much fun finding our own personal styles!

…But let's try to avoid floundering, slipping on uphills, or straining!

A fun thing to do in a second class is to have yourself videotaped then tape the instructor skiing the same section then explain what you're both doing. You'll often have an "ah-ha!" experience and surprise awareness of what you need to do once you SEE yourself skiing. "Oh, THAT'S why I'm slipping!" It's also great for fine-tuning. It's fun! …Tape, review, try again! Maybe tape again to make sure you've adjusted. It can be really hard to change! (Even a second taping sometimes has folks slapping their head. "I thought I totally changed, yet I look the same!)

Learners should be able to have fun every step of the way -- so I don't go for awkward static drills. I do have some drills and dryland movements, but they don't last long and they're designed to include some fun.

I teach a wide range of people, from never-evers to advanced. I glean what works best from all the sources available. Sure, we'll make serious efforts and sometimes you have to try hard. But I emphasize fun and play like I don't see elsewhere -- even though these aspects are absolutely needed for XC to become popular! I think it's because typical how-to emphasizes racing and a Type-A personality. I confess, sometimes we'll be corny.

When considering what to learn and where to learn it, classic stride skiing is the all-round type of skiing that you can do anywhere. For ski-skating you need a wide machine-groomed course or firm crust -- make sure you have these conditions before learning to skate.

Class Clothes

Most people wear too much to their first class. And what they wear is too shiny and everything-proof. Skiing keeps you warm. In a class you will stand around a bit and be less vigorous, but you'll still heat up! Wear layers and bring a little pack to stash your excess -- or just toss it over a tree branch for the time being. You'll only need windproof snow-pants type gear if it's really cold and windy. For falling and getting snowy, just keep brushing yourself off (have a friend help).

Generally for skiing you wear less than if you go out for a winter walk. You should start out feeling chilly. In 10 minutes that should change to nicely warm. Try see how little you can wear and be comfy. Overheating in skiing is a much bigger nuisance and is far more likely than getting cold. Getting hot actually makes it hard to think and discourages you from moving! Wearing too much definitely gets in the way.

It's fun learning how skiing changes your body's energy levels as you warm up on an outing. (Hint: it turns you into a furnace.) Light/med wool is best for everything, from head to toe and skin to wind, but most anything is fine. Jeans are fine! (Especially flannel-lined jeans!)

Treats!

For your beginner lesson FOR SURE BRING SNACKS AND A BEV! Apple juice rules! Wine is pretty good, too. After each phase of your lesson, have a snack and a sip! No skimping! A pause and a sip lets it sink in. If you string it all together it can become an overwhelming blur.

We are like dogs in an obedience class. Every time we learn something we are going to reward ourselves!

Basics

We get the 3 good things I keep listing simply by weighting, unweighting and extra-weighting (bouncing, pouncing, flexing, kicking, pushing) -- it works like alpine skiing, ice skating, and skateboarding. Any kind of scooter.

Weighting means we're standing on our skis – and gliding. Unweighting by jumping up or putting all weight on one ski lets us easily move a ski or both skis around. Extra-weighting from dropping down lets us kick down (or to the side in skating) and gives the propulsion.

Speed doesn't matter. (It's relative. If you feel a breeze in your hair or you say "whee!" on the downhill, you're good.) What you look like doesn't matter.

Casual skiing looks different from racing. But it's good to know the full range because sometimes race moves come in handy for everyone. But casual skiers take it easy and often do things that add more to fun and easiness than to speed – so don't judge the one by the other. Use what works for you. You'll likely use a mix of both on every outing.

In particular, the kind of skiing that people do most and the places where they do it are both totally different from racing. Trail Skiing and Ski Touring are what we'll focus on coz that's what 90% of people do 90% of the time. Race technique helps mostly on the uphills or when the going

gets tough and you need to focus on physics. Fun delivers the results the rest of the time. We'll cover both.

How Skis Work

The thing with striding is that to get grip and power the foot stops for an instant, grips, and you leap forward off of the stopped foot.

Why does a classic ski grip? It has sticky wax or a textured pattern under the middle portion of the ski. The ski also has a camber or arch to it. When you're just standing on the ski, with half your weight on it, as when gliding down a hill, or even with all your weight on it -- the sticky part under your foot is OFF the snow. There is less pressure on it, anyway. Then when you drop down a bit and flex your ankle and knee then stand UP again you suddenly put MORE than your body weight on the ski and this presses the grip part into the snow and it grips! It only takes a little more increase in your weight to make this happen. Swinging up with your hand at the same time that you straighten your leg also helps you press down more.

It's important to realize that the grip-zone is centered around the pivot point of your binding: around the ball of your foot. It's not equally centered around your whole foot. That is, it goes farther forward than it goes to the rear. So when you press down with the BALL of your foot, that's when you grip. When you're shoving forward with your glide foot and have weight on the HEEL of your foot the camber has less weight on it and you glide.

So it's good to feel where the weight

is on your feet as they stride fore and aft. Getting a feel for that will help you both grip and glide.

The leg and arm actions and posture of classic ski-striding and ski-skating are the same -- just with skating the kick is to the side -- only difference! With skating the foot never stops gliding. That's why it's faster. But the sideways motion reduces the efficiency of skating due to the tangential direction. Skating also seems easier to learn than striding, at least on moderate terrain. The net effect is that skating is about 25% faster for learners. As you become more skilled the speeds of the two modes get closer together. (Elite skaters are only about 10% faster than striders.) Also, when stride-skis are waxed just right their gripwax really doesn't slow them down, especially in klister conditions when only a small amount of wax is used.

The challenge in stride-skiing is there's less tolerance for messing-up. If your butt is back in ski-skating, you just work harder, but you can still get around and especially (kind of sort of) up hills. If you don't have a bit of forward posture in striding and flex that ankle to get grip, then you can't ski up hills hardly at all -- and you'll suffer and hate it or just bail out on skiing and start to trot or herringbone.

Thankfully, learning to get grip in classic-striding is easy. But it isn't intuitive! ...Which is why self-taught skiers almost always suffer on uphills and work harder elsewhere, too. (I often see the ski marks of skiers who glide along until they get to any tiny uphill where they immediately bail out and start to herringbone.)

Start at the Start

Find a flat section of packed trail about 50 yards long where you're going to do your learning. It should be near a gentle hill and a medium hill.

Now practice the ready stance: stand like a wrestler or gun-slinger. Hands forward. Knees and ankles lightly bent. Shoulders slumped. Chin down a bit so neck is neutral, not tense. Weight evenly on your feet, but maybe a bit forward toward the balls.

Here's a super way to get into the position that will be awesome for all your skiing: Stand. Jump. Try to land without making a sound. Land as soft as you can. See? You land in a dropped position with flexed ankles and knees and hands poised a bit low and in front. Very cool!

Now take a STEP FORWARD and stand on one foot with a slight forward tilt of torso and let your rear leg float/lift slightly up off the ground and hang there. The leg you're standing on has the knee and ankle bent a bit and in tension but calm -- do this both feet.

Learn a Lot Just Standing there!

Time for more dryland motions:

First, do a few calisthenics. Swing your arms, bend your waist, toe-touch, limber up.

Now swing your arms fore and aft, bent 45 degrees, let them fling, relaxed, lead with front of hand, make a motion like tossing cup of water down trail in front of you.

Now while you're standing there swinging your arms add in a bounce. As you swing your hands and your hands pass your thighs give a bounce like you're standing on a bathroom scale and trying to make it weigh more than you weigh. Flex those knees and ankles! Drop down with each arm swing. It's good for you.

Almost Ready to Ski!

We're going to do a couple simple things to start that will make everything else come together easily.

First, practice clicking into your skis IN-DOORS. Maybe don't even put your boots on. Use your hands to click-in the boots -- learn how your bindings work!

Now go outside wearing your ski boots and with your ski gear, but put it all aside. Just walk around. Swing your arms like you might when walking or running. Normally. Don't think about it. If you think about it, you'll likely do the opposite swing timing that you normally do. So walk and swing. Put a little pep in your step. Swing your arms big and long, swing them bent. Jog a bit and swing them. This is the same arm swing you'll use skiing. Do this for a minute. This will start to implant proper arm action into your brain before you complicate things with the poles and skis. Don't skip it! In fact, if you ever feel yourself bogging down or freezing-up with your arm/leg timing in your learning just ditch your skis and poles and walk and jog around again for a tiny minute to "reset" your natural motions. It'll then be easier to keep doing it when you ski. (This is sometimes an emergency intervention I make, with a laugh, when instructing. I'll see a skier gradually slowing and staring and realize they're catching a brain-freeze!

Time for a reset...)

Now practice stepping forward again. Let the back foot just hang there. Now try standing and tipping forward and catching yourself with one foot stepped out a couple feet. Notice the flex in that front knee and ankle. Just relax out on that front foot with all your weight on it. Flex a little. And let the back foot hang or touch the ground.

Jump up and land without a sound: there's our posture!

Now put on the poles. Hand up thru, then grab down onto strap and pole. (Some poles have cuff-like straps. Have someone show you how they work.)

Adjust the length of the strap so that the web of your hand between your thumb and forefinger is at the pivot point of where the strap goes into the ski pole grip. You want the strap to be able to keep the pole on your hand and to take a lot of the load of poling and you don't want to have to grip the pole very hard at all.

But! This is just one of several ways to use a pole strap! It is the 100% official way. And you should do it this way 95% of the time. ...But what if your hand gets a little numb sometime. (Straps can pinch a little now'n'then.) Or what if you're skiing in deep snow and suddenly your poles feel a little long? ...Using a variety of grips can help. Put your hand through the strap and grab the pole like a rookie: sometimes this is good! For something different, grab one side of the strap plus pole. Or just hook your thumb through the bottom of the strap! These options all vary the height of your poling or change how the strap presses on your hand.

Ski Walking

Now we're going to pretend like we're skiing with our poles on and skis off. Find some firm ground for this. Actually, you can do this anytime, like in the autumn. Walk around timing your striding with your poling just as if you were swinging your arms as you walked: this is Nordic Walking. Now bound a bit, keeping your feet close to the ground and pole with each bound: This is very close to Nordic Skiing! (I remember a Russian coach saying you can readily imitate skiing to 95% exactness just while walking in the grass.) Walking with poles teaches you to time your leg action with your arm action. Just doing this TEACHES you a lot about skiing!

The casual touring stride is fine, but it is characterized by LATE POLING. This is a problem on uphills. Ski-walking without skis instills you with the right timing so that you know how to do it when you need it! ...Do this for a minute.

Skis On!

Now let's put our skis on in the snow. Stand next to the skis and make sure snow isn't clogging the binding. A few kicks at the binding just behind the bar-slot should clear your boot. Most bindings you can just step into and press and they will click. But you might have to press the button with your pole tip. If a boot won't click in, scrape under the boot-bar with a pole-tip. After one boot clicks in, kick other boot into the back of the clicked-in boot.

Since you're new to using your gear in the snow this clicking-in might be a pain in the butt. It gets better.

In XC skiing we use two methods to turn. One way is with our tips going outward. The other is with our tips inward and our tails swinging outward.

Also, the main way we move our skis is by stepping them around. We lift them up and put them down where we want them. We can't skid them as much as we can in alpine skiing. To move our skis around we have to stand on one ski then move the unweighted ski. Let's get comfy with this!

So, with our skis on, let's do some circles. Keeping your tails close to each other step in a circle in a fan shape, around and around. Both directions. This teaches turning. You'll also skate-ski with your tips pointed away from each other in a Vee.

Now, keeping your tips pointed to each other step in a star-pattern circle by leading with your heels, each way. This gets you comfy with sticking out a heel. This will be how you brake while skiing. You'll do a snowplow skid by stepping out onto a ski that is shoved with it's heel out to the side, tilting it inward then weighting it so it skids.

Forward tilt with flex and relaxed rear leg float on left. Still feeling it out on the right. (photo courtesy Crosscut Mt Sports)

Bend the knees! Bend the knees! ...The wipeout is mere moments away. Instead, let's flex the ankles...and bend the knees. Get ready! (The hands are good!)

Ski in circles -- skate stepping both ways -- try to scooter -- angle your outside ski outward and scooter off it and turn left (or right) around and around. Use your poles for balance if you like -- you can have some glide on both skis.

Now, put your skis parallel and step to the sides a few times each way. Also try to flip your skis around one at a time to do a 180-degree about-face.

I'm Falling!

Since you're going to fall, probably soon (if you haven't already), let's learn how. What you want to do is to try to fall a bit back and to the side -- on a butt cheek. Avoid pitching forward! When in doubt, plop back and to the side. Falling is OK! The ground is soft in skiing and our skis won't hurt us. Also, when you fall try to fling your poles back. Don't let them jam. (It's amazing how easy it is to kind of organize yourself before you fall.) So just tip over right now. Now, let's get up. There's only one way to do it: get your poles on either side of you pointed back and sort out your skis side by side going across any slope then get your hands on the ground toward the front of you and put one knee

up and one knee down pointing forward. Push off the ground with a hand. Your hands and knees should be aimed toward the front of your skis. Your heels are free and you can pivot at your toes. It's OK if your rear foot is twisted a bit but don't stress it much. Put most weight on a level, flat front foot. If you try to push with your hands toward the rear half of the skis you won't be able to get up. Be careful using your poles: our shoulders are weak when our hands work above them. And poles are weak under side-loads. Mostly use your feet to stand back up. Steady with a pole if need be.

You've done so much already! It's time for a little break! ...Eat a little treat and have something to drink. You're learning! Each step is a big deal. No need to rush any of it. You're programming your brain. It's work! Take it in small pieces. Let each one sink in.

Skiing! ...Well, the Lower Half!

Now put both poles aside and find a flat place of packed snow (or a ski track) about 50 feet long and click into just ONE ski. Put both poles aside.

Scooter back and forth on the one ski pushing off with your boot. You don't have to glide hardly at all. Just walk and scooter. Glide a little if you like. No need to get into a balancing contest. Try to propel yourself in two ways: *kick with your boot repeatedly while standing on the ski, like it's a skateboard; *plant your boot in the snow and swing the ski past it then glide on the ski. The second way is how we will ski most of the time. Skiing isn't skateboarding, but it's neat to feel both ways we can propel ourselves.

Scooter back'n'forth. Flex your legs more and less and see what that does. Do this scootering for a minute then change feet.

Now put both skis on. Still leave your poles aside. On our 50-yard stretch of flat trail, let's ski along without poles. Just swing your arms fore and aft in time with your legs. Use natural, opposite timing just as if you were walking or running. Don't do bear-walking! When learners overthink it, or even when they're first just trying to comprehend what's happening to them, they will very often start to kick and pole on the same side. Nope! We pole with one hand and stride with the opposite foot. (If you start to mess up, take off poles and skis and walk/jog around to "reset.")

To get some grip as you swing along, visualize pressing each pushing-knee down to the area of the ski in front of the binding. Push when your weight is centered over the ski then step forward to the other ski.

You should find that as you swing an arm forward and your hand goes up that you can "set" the opposite foot into the snow and it won't slip and you can swing the other foot past it.

If it does slip, lower yourself more deeply as you swing along. The more you flex your ankle and knee the more grip you should feel as you then straighten them. Same with the swinging arm: the lower it is as it swings past your thigh and the higher and faster it swings up, the more you'll be able to "plant" your gripping ski.

Try to recoil off of one foot and get a good glide onto the other foot. But it's not

a backward kick at all. Your goal is to keep the "kicking" foot planted. I guess that makes it a misnomer to call it a kicking foot. A pole is easy to "plant." Your goal is to similarly plant your opposite foot! You actually kick your gliding foot forward. That is the true kicking foot. You are "posting" off of the planted foot and pole and swinging the free leg and pole forward with vigor.

Play around with big arm motions and big leg action and then also with compact arm motions, keeping your arms bent and close to you and making your motions have more 'flick' to them. All the combinations of big and little arm and leg motions are fun to try. The hand motion flicks to the rear. It's not like pulling a rope.

Swing, swing, swing! Try every kind of timing you can think of. Kick and freeze the glide. Hang it out there just to feel it. Then compare that to a constant "ebb and flow" sort of motion. In our real skiing we'll do a smooth, pulsing motion with no static part.

Now also do it up and down a very slight grade so you can feel it going faster down a hill and having to be more precise and with sharper bounces to get back up a hill.

Ski back'n'forth without poles for a few minutes.

Many elite skiers ski without their poles for a couple minutes before an outing. They'll even ski up moderate hills.

You may be itching to "go skiing" but this preliminary half hour of bouncing, walking around, arm swinging, and laying on the ground is critical! It's highly unlikely you'd

Skiing in the Ready Position. Good for skate, stride, up, down, all around.

be able to get your skis to grip so that you can enjoy gliding UP a hill if you try to skip any of these things. They are all critical for imprinting your brain for ski fun.

In XC skiing, grip is what makes our glide! Everything we do is designed to get you comfy with what it takes to grip. Glide isn't our concern at all. It is a side effect. If we can get you gripping up a hill, it will be a total success!

And for the rest of the time -- descending and turning -- good body position is required just to stay standing up! ...And for everything else!

Time for another snack and a sip!

A Bit More Skiing -- Upper Half!

Put your poles back on! (Hand up thru, grab down onto strap and pole.)

By the way, your poles are sized about right when you're standing on the ground

and they come to your armpits or your shoulders. When you're in your skis they'll be a couple inches lower.

Your best pole length can vary depending on where you'll ski most: if you're in the hills then a bit shorter poles are handy. If you live where it's flat then an inch or two longer are nice. If you'll be touring in deeper snow, or skiing homemade trails in places where it snows a lot, then if the poles are sinking in a lot you'll like them longer, but if the tracks are set deep and the snow on the sides is firm you might like them shorter than usual!

To pole, plant the basket near your feet, maybe an inch behind them.

Your hands should be in front of you, close to you, with your arms bent about 90 degrees when they plant. When you push you'll drop your weight slightly onto the poles in a bit of a 'crunch' action and you'll push your hands at your baskets until your hands are just past your hips. Then you'll let up but still "flick" your hands through until your arms extend behind you. Then you kind of whip your hands back forward. (When you doublepole, you'll ab-crunch more.)

It's OK if your hands are a few inches more in front of you or out to your sides but in those cases they are being used more like outriggers, for balance more than propulsion. Also, if you plant your basket in front of your foot, note that whenever you push down on a handle and the basket is right below that handle your force is support, not propulsion. Your poles only help you move if the baskets are BEHIND the grips -- if they are angled to the rear and if your hands are somewhat close to your body. As your hand pushes back and your arm straightens, your hands drop lower. If your arms have a good bend in them then your upper body, back and torso-weight can help you pole. If you just use your arms you will be weaker and get tired much more quickly. When striding your upper body might not bob very much but it can still be adding to your poling. Even when doublepoling, you don't always drop the torso very much, but your torso and abs can add even more than when striding.

You can practice double-poling on a flat or slight downhill using only your upper body and not your arms by getting into a track and holding your arms fully bent and tight against your body. Now just make little rocking crunches of your torso. Drop your knees a bit for power then stand up to recover. You can pole along pretty well like this, not using any arm action at all.

It's good to tilt forward a bit as you plant your poles and to "fall onto" your pole-straps. This works even more for double-poling. It gives power and is efficient posture. To do this, try to deepen your ankle bend and slightly increase your knee flex. Sometimes people bend at the waist as they try to get forward lean. We want more of a whole-body "tip."

I've seen people plant their pole baskets in FRONT of their grip. It can be fun to swing your poles a lot and this forward-plant works for them like a "feeler." They get stability from it. But when they plant like that and press with their hand, for the first part of their motion they are actually pushing themselves backward. They are impeding their forward motion. A moment later their push is going straight down and so the force is pushing them up to the sky: again, fine as a prop but zero propulsion. Only when the basket is behind the grip does poling help us move. It's natural to first use poles as outriggers. But our no-poles practice skiing should help us see we don't always need poles as props. When sight-seeing and not paying attention, poles-as-feelers is fine. When you want easy gliding, though, you know what to do!

Poling is all one smooth motion. We put weight on the pole at first when it's a bit more vertical then tilt the grip down and forward and keep adding power. The first weighting is called the 'loading' -- it's when our poles bend the most. You can really 'pop' the poles at this time and the rest of the action can just be a whipping thru of the hands. But propulsion happens when the pole is tilted. Make sure you're still giving good power to the poles as they come close to your hips. You can ease up on them at that point. When you're enjoying nice long glide you can let your pole-hands fly WAY to the back and let go of the grips except for maybe your thumb and forefinger. Your straps will keep your poles from getting too wild.

When you go up a slight hill notice how falling onto your poles and an ab-crunch really helps with doublepoling. Also notice that you will shorten-up and choke up on your poling motion when going up a hill. Adjust these things to keep the glide going and avoid bogging down. You want steady gliding, not a yo-yo type of flow.

Penny's first time skiing featured this awesome moment of paralyzing laughter. Here she is taking a breather and admiring the sky after a remarkable layback tumble.

Remember, as you whip your "off" hand (or both hands) back to the front and up they're actually helping you set your kick wax to get grip (as when striding or doing the kick doublepole). It's pretty neat!

HAVE ANOTHER SQUIRT OF APPLE JUICE AND A SNACK!

Finally... Real Skiing!

First let's learn how to turn. Your star-shaped ski practicing will serve you now. To make a turn that's kind of fast you just step around it, skating out on one foot, or just weighting the outer foot, then moving your unweighted inner foot to the inside in the new direction then standing on that and bringing the unweighted outside foot back in to meet the inside foot. The tips move away from each other. This is called a skate or step turn. Find a turn and practice! Turning will teach you about weighting

and unweighting -- and this will help your ability to get good grip!

On uphill turns or in tighter situations you may want to step the inside ski into the turn then lift your heel and swing the tail of the outside ski outward and keep the tip down and near where it was before then swing that outside ski forward and alongside the inner ski. In this case the tail swings out wide while the tip keeps pointing where you want to go. This is called a striding or swing turn. You can actually keep the striding and gliding going throughout this turn. It is beautiful, feels good, and is effective. The skate/step turn is less efficient in some situations, especially on an uphill turn. Also, very often if you get off the trail or into the shrubbery, or when getting up from a fall, you may want to "extract" your skis to get them untangled and back in order. Being comfy with swinging your ski tails is key -- and fun!

You can only do things with skis in three ways. When the skis are: weighted, un-weighted, or extra-weighted.

If you lock up and straighten your legs they won't be able to be unweighted or extra-weighted, so you won't be able to move them around easily.

Get used to stepping around and lifting your skis and moving them from side to side by weighting one ski and unweighting the other.

On downhills we can turn by weighting and extra-weighting our skis and skidding, snowplowing or carving, but even there, unweighting lets us get set up.

To start to get comfy on downhills, here's our next super skill... Find an easy downhill. Do your "quiet jump" at the top to get ready to glide down. Then practice stepping from foot to foot and moving from side to side as you go down. Do that a few times. If there's a turn in the down-hill practice shuffling your feet to get around it. (We'll snowplow more later.)

In classic skiing when you flex down a bit in knee and ankle then leap off of the ball of your foot you get grip. The subtle-ness is in keeping that stopped foot grip-ping. If we flex our ankle and knee we can be nicely subtle.

It's fun to play with striding. It's what you'll do the most. Find the way you like to go. You're looking for your personal style and rhythm. You'll also want to change your style to adapt to the trail and snow conditions. Sometimes it's hard and fast, other times it's soft and slow. It can change back and forth in a short distance so you'll find your style adapting to fit. Try long and low, reaching out, stretching out. Try stand-ing tall and keeping your hands near your shoulders -- that's a good way when you're moving fast, big on the glide. Change it up as you go. Different styles use different muscles. Now and then we need to rest some and use others. One of the funnest things about skiing is flowing through the transitions, mixing up your ski moves to find the most fun.

Up We Go!

To first learn how to ski up a hill, just jog up it. This will also reinforce good arm action. Use your arms like when you're jogging. As you trot from foot to foot you'll be putting 100% of your weight on each and as you jump forward you'll put even more than your bodyweight on the ski for an instant -- then the gripwax will grip. Hold yourself in place with your pole and up you go. Shorten-up to go up.

Try light flicky moves -- on the uphills but also on the flats. Ski around a bit both up and down, skiing lightly and making sure you don't bog down.

Then stretch out and put more into it. Pounce like a puma! Drive your foot up the hill. As your hands and feet all come together, feel yourself coiling up. Then pounce out!

But feel how you have to choke it up a bit as you go uphill. Don't pole as far back or reach as far forward.

When you kick it's more like you're kicking a ball forward down the trail with the other foot! The forward driving leg is a more definite action than the rearward. That's because to kick you have to STOP your foot. You set the kick wax, get grip, then swing and drive your other leg past it and forward. It also helps to think about driving forward with your opposite hand.

Feeling out what works for a climb takes sensitivity. The firmness of the track affects what works. Sometimes going up in a firm track means standing taller and shorten-ing up your arm-action, getting punchier, and shoving your foot further forward. But if the track is soft, or you're feeling the skis start to slip you might "crouch" your way up the whole hill in a low, dropped posture, so you don't miss a kick.

It's fun to see how steep of a hill you can ski up before resorting to the herringbone. Good skiers can keep a glide going up quite a steep hill. It's fun on a hill where you see the marks of everyone else herringboning and you can just stride your way up. Of course, you don't want to be able to do this just because you have such sticky skis that they aren't gliding. Everyone finds a waxing and skiing style that suits them best. I like to ski so that I glide a lot up hills, but not everyone does. Some just jog up hills. Typically jogging is more work than gliding, but it can be fast and if that's what you like go for it! (Young Klaebo is winning World Cup races these days with an uphill running style: but on slightly less steep climbs he glides beautifully.)

The Drop

Here's a trick you won't find taught very often... Everybody now and then slips and misses a kick going up a hill. It's gonna happen. It's a balancing act. If a ski is too grippy it doesn't glide its best. If it glides too fast you will find that it has no grip for an uphill. The best ski, though, has nearly perfect glide while still giving perfect grip when your technique is spot on. Also, you will also be skiing as a balancing act: if you pounce a lot you'll get more grip but it's easier to just flow so you'll adjust your technique to the steepness of the uphill: and you'll screw up and suddenly

Touring stride. Upright. Good for looking around or wearing a pack. Not for uphills. Short poling. Late kick. Rear leg doesn't float as much.

find that you were too casual at some point and you'll feel your ski start to slip. So both things are going to happen: you are going to slip, and sometimes you'll feel that you're STARTING to slip. What you do in either case is the same: DROP! Get lower. This will mean only an inch or two of drop. Flex your ankles more deeply. Lower your hands. Crouch. Sometimes on a steep climb it feels like my hands get kinda close to the ground when I do the Drop. This may well give enough extra grip to let your ski work. It's fun!

This will also give your NEXT kick a better chance of sticking. ...It happens in an instant.

HAVE A SQUIRT OF APPLE JUICE AND A SNACK!!!

Land the Plane

As you stride along you might start hearing that your rear ski is slapping down behind you. It can get pretty loud! This happens because you're not standing up enough on your glide ski nor are you shoving through enough with the glide ski. It also happens because your toes aren't pointing down the trail. Lift with your toes. And bring that foot back thru under your hips like it's an airplane hitting a landing strip. Then the ski will have a SOFT, quiet landing -- which also is fast. The ski should touch down right when it comes under your hips or maybe even in front of them. Drive for the glide!

The Touring Stride

Here's a big concept not explained elsewhere. ...There's a time for letting your rear ski come back to earth farther back. Or for hardly letting your ski come off the ground to begin with!

Now, we're never intentionally doing stuff with our back ski as it's going back. It's all just side effects of kick and of the position of our body and the flex of our ankles. That's why if you do my base move of just standing on one foot and flexing your ankle and tilting forward a bit your rear leg will tend to outrigger a bit to the rear: it doesn't take work that's just where it goes to balance you. The more you tilt, the farther back the rear leg goes. You don't force it.

If we're skiing with a rucksack on a soft homestyle trail that's a bit uneven and if we're scouting the countryside we might have an UPRIGHT posture. In this case, as you kick your leg won't go back very far and it might come down quite soon. Sometimes having both skis on the snow more lets you keep a better feel for the trail -- especially if you're not paying attention. This is the essence of Ski Touring and striding on flat terrain. A lot of time fitness skiers will start doublepoling when it gets flat, but if you want to keep striding and look around you'll do the Touring Stride.

Your poling is also greatly affected by your orientation. If you're looking around, carrying a pack, skiing on a soft trail, your poles may well be placed a bit out farther to your sides and if you're standing upright they will probably get planted farther ahead and with straighter arms.

This is because you're using the poles for some support! They're a bit more like outrigger or feelers now. You're watching the trail less. We're only talking a couple inches here. If your arms are way forward or way out well, that's bad: we don't need much Frankenstein in our style. But using poles for stability is great! With an upright posture our poling will also stop sooner: right at the hip. If you try to shove them farther back you'll just end up arching your back backwards and making your low back concave -- and tire it out.

If tour-skiers who have an upright posture try to kick too far back or pole too far back they'll tend to get sore backs and let them down soon. Low back fatigue isn't what we want.

I note this style isn't taught or encouraged. It's largely labeled a mistake by the pro's. ...And this oversight is an example of race-bias in instruction.

At the same time, this style of skiing won't work to get grip up a hill! This is Flats Striding. Once you get to an uphill, you'll need to get punchy and flex your

Here's monster herringbone up a very steep climb at our favorite local ungroomed singletrack trail system. Top skills for this difficult move. No bail-out waddling here! Behind him a skier is skidaddling up the side of the gullied part of the climb where herringbone would back-slide.

ankles and shorter your poling to get grip.

And here's something more to consider, if your brain has room by this point: You'll also adjust your skiing to fit your equipment in addition to the trail condition. If you're using race gear on a groomed trail you'll benefit from paying close attention to your wax and your wax pocket (grip-zone) -- if you hit it just right you'll have both total grip and perfect glide. You'll probably dial in on a punchier style where you kick in a very crisp way then relax as you glide on the firm, flat track. Poling will also be quicker, with a "pop" followed by a float. By contrast, if you use older, heavier, flexier gear -- such as wood skis and bamboo poles -- you'll probably tend toward a longer, lower, swoopier style. It's all good!

STOP FOR A SQUIRT OF APPLE JUICE AND A SNACK!!!

The Full Enchilada

Skiing has "gears" just like biking. So here are the 6 gears of striding from little to big: herringbone > race striding > striding doublepole > kick doublepole > (tour striding) > doublepole .

It's time to learn the "big gears" -- the doublepole moves.

When you're on the flats and gliding fast, or even on a slight downhill, you might be going too fast for your feet to help so you'll just use poles.

Doublepole

We've already gone through the doublepole basics, but here's more: reach forward with bent arms, plant your baskets near your feet, then collapse your weight onto the straps, then do a little ab-crunch and rocker your arms down toward your hips. Straighten your arms as they approach your hips and even more so after your hips. Your hand pushing aims to the baskets. You kind of 'whip' your hands. You don't need to bob up and down a whole lot but it will be more so than with striding.

You can compare a lot of torso drop to just a little. And depending on your glide speed you can shorten or lengthen your poling action.

The fast guys find it helps to recover your poles with your elbows kind of sticking out. This helps flick the poles back forward. Then when you plant your poles if you keep that kind of "flared" style you might be able to use your lats more. Feel it and see what you think. They also "wham" the poles down hard. That first "catch" moment is a good place to put most of your work. ...Especially if you feel that it works for you! Remember, efficiency in one place and for one person doesn't always translate everywhere.

A really cool thing about doublepoling is that you can get into it as a rhythm. A lot of people think it's boring because it's only half of a skiing action. There's no legwork. Well, it's a bit like canoeing and we like paddling, right? A way to bring interest into DPing is to get the breath involved. You don't want to force a pattern but it can't hurt to use your motions to assist your breathing. So when you first 'hit' the forward hands, at first just hang from the poles, and let your belly sag and exhale --

Swing-tail or Striding Turn. For wonderful flow and feeling of transition continuity.

'woof!' then tighten and do the ab-crunch / curl and finish emptying your lungs. Then when you stand up really breathe in. Then again with a really nice big relaxed full exhale during the poling. I find that this turns DPing into something that I could do all day.

Actually legs do get plenty of work in doublepoling -- just like they can in canoe or kayak paddling if we're bracing our feet. As you drop onto your poles and your hands go past your hips you'll be flexing and bending your legs. Then as you recover you'll be standing up again. That takes work!

Now we'll learn a couple more DP moves.

Kick-Doublepole

The kick-doublepole is also done when the gliding is easy and fast, but not as fast as when just only DPing. Indeed, you can do it up a bit of an uphill. What you do is as your hands come forward together from a doublepole move you flex your knees and ankles and "gather up" as your hands come forward past your legs. Then as your hands are rising up, you kick down with one foot. That kick lets you really reach out far. It shoves your weight out there more over your hands so when you pole again it has more umph. Then as you drive your hands back past your hips, you drive that foot forward again. Then the same foot can kick again or you can alternate feet. Again, if the foot slaps down loudly at the back think about "landing the plane" as you drive that foot forward, also flex more in the glide ankle and stand up more in a forward tilt. ...And, again, if you're doing this move on the flats, while wearing a pack, in soft snow, you might be more upright and the rear foot might naturally come down sooner but just try to keep things smooth.

This move is basically like scootering with one leg -- the other foot keeps riding the "scooter."

This is a great move for practicing getting your hips forward. You kick yourself out over your poles. You have to catch yourself with your poles to not fall. It's fun! It teaches commitment.

Striding Doublepole

Now we come to a cool thing. It's a new ski move that I'm promoting. Actually, it's not new -- what is? But it doesn't officially exist and I'm the only one doing something about it. It's called the Striding Doublepole. It's a kind of doublepole that's real easy. It doesn't involve moving the torso very much and you don't need a lot of speed or power. It's also great for when the glide isn't that fast for whatever reason, including that you're just taking it easy. But on soft trails or when carrying a pack, it's just the ticket! It's the kind of doublepoling that works up the steeper hills. So you might do it just before you have to start striding or you'll bog down. So you kick as

The Drop saves the day when you lose grip or miss a kick.

you bring your hands forward past your hips then you kick again as you doublepole down back past your hips. In short, your legs are striding just as in stride-skiing only you're only poling for one of the strides and the poling is doublepoling. It's two-hands action every other stride, but both feet are striding.

For regular kick doublepoling one foot stays still and gliding all the time. But the trail might not be fast enough for that so you'll want to use that leg, too, sometimes -- so feel free to do just that! I note that this technique isn't in print anywhere or officially taught anywhere, but it's a wonderful move! It's actually an old technique from back in the wood ski days. It's also a move that many Tour Skiers have stumbled across on their own when they were just feeling lazy or like changing up their striding. I've even had a Tour Skier tell me "Yeah, it's probably all wrong, but I like doing it!" No, it's all good!

I also note that the poling and kicking action is the same as with the most popular ski-skate move, the V1. It's kinda neat how they're the same. Indeed if you change the timing of the pole-side kicking in the Striding Doublepole so that the kick happens right with the poling, you can do it up quite a steep uphill, just as if you were V1 skating. Then if you delay the kick the Striding Doublepole becomes more like the V2A or Open Field skate move and is nicely suitable for flat, fast terrain -- just like the V2A.

Pendulum Poling

Back in the wood ski days, the skis, poles and boots were heavier and trails were much less likely to be groomed. That hasn't entirely changed. Touring skis and poles are heavier than racing skis, and there are still a lot of wood skis in play. When skiing home-style trails, you need more options for the wide variety of conditions encountered, so let's work to expand our moves to fit our needs. It's a win-win all around.

Sometimes people say cross-country skiing isn't as popular as it could be because it's too complicated. I doubt that. Do skateboarding and snowboarding have too many moves? People love variety. The real problem is that what's taught and sold doesn't fit new skiers' needs well enough.

Skiers are often out there with a passel of friends rather than racing. So don't they need to learn how to ski in close quarters just like racers? They also want to keep their flow, yet not run up on each other's

Yay, crashing!

It means you're trying.

Fall back and to the side whenever you can. Then get skis together and below you, pointed across fall-line. Poles both pointing back. One knee up. ...And up!

Striding Doublepole. Clockwise from any.

tails.

An easy way do this is by pendulum poling, a move you won't find taught elsewhere.

A skier gliding up behind another wants to slow down without losing their rhythm. They can do this by skipping a pole plant on one or both sides while swinging the basket forward but pumping the hand back toward the chest. By the time the pole swings back, it's time to pole again. It lets you skip a poling (and maybe slow down a bit) while keeping your same rhythm.

I use this move a lot when kick double poling on a flat touring trail amidst a group of friends. Our speeds will tend to diverge as we flow over little humps. By using pendulum poling, I keep my rhythm and my gap constant to the skier ahead of me.

Anyway, all these moves are easy! It's fun to just realize they exist. You don't have to worry about them or even remember them when you're first beginning. At some point, though, they'll all show back up to help you have fun when you need them! Certainly don't stress out over any of the details. We're just playing around here! Mostly it'll be great if we can just get you comfy with all the basics and get a feel for handling your skis around and for gripping and gliding. ...For crashing and getting back up and such.

Herringbone

You'll often enough find an uphill that's too steep to get any grip up. Well, to get up it easily we do what is called the Herringbone. That's where you stick your ski tips out to each side, or, really, you just rotate the ski outward at the front and the tail rotates inward at the rear. You set the ski down at an angle to the direction of the uphill. Then you tilt your knee in to bite the edge. You do this when your wax will no longer grip. But you don't change anything else about what you do! You flex your ankle deeply and you reach up the hill a bit with your other hand, arm bent. Then you trot up the hill! You keep your keep mostly moving just forward and back. You don't waddle! Sometimes when it's really steep you move more from side to side. But really the skis should move entirely over and past each other before they set down. So they're at an angle but they don't hit each other. It's fun! Take your time. Don't try to step too far. Keep your poles set with the baskets to the rear and behind you! Don't reach too far forward. Try to keep yourself doing the same as always. Light, relaxed. Don't work too hard -- it's a steep hill! The trick is to not waddle and not lift your skis very much -- only enough to have the one ski pass over the other.

If the hill is too steep even for herringboning, then put your skis totally sideways and sidestep up the hill -- or down the hill if you don't want to descend it in another way.

The awesome and mighty Skidaddle. Best (only) way to ski up a gullied-out hill!

Gliding Herringbone

Here's a fun skill. It's also illegal! Yep, don't try it in a Classic race. You'll get DQed. It's pure classic but someone might think you're Skating, which isn't allowed. No one else is going to explain it to you even though it's nifty.

If you slip when climbing and want to herringbone, try to not switch over totally at first, take a herringbone stride and then another but glide out onto that ski! It's doing classic skiing to the sides. Pointing the ski to the side and edging it gives the wax a better chance to grip so you are still stopping the ski and gripping with it and then kicking off of it and gliding onto the other ski.

The slope of the hill is less when you angle a ski out. So you have a chance for easier grip.

With normal herringbone you trot and stop with each stride and get no glide. But very often you still CAN get some glide!

The real rule-breaking is if you glide WHILE kicking: then that is skating! But the rule says "glide only when skis are parallel or in direction of travel." ...Even if you are NOT skating. The snag is that an official couldn't easily see the difference from a distance. The gliding herringbone is fun, helpful and instructive. Just don't do it in a classic race!

Skidaddle

Here's a trick that our gang has developed for ourselves and which I haven't seen hinted at elsewhere. I suppose others must know it, but I bet this is the first book to promote it. We call it the Skidaddle. So, what do you do if your uphill is eroded? What if your trail has a U-shape to it? A lot of trails do have eroded sections. What happens when you try to herringbone such terrain? You splay your tips as usual -- yet the ski slips down toward the center of the gully on you! By rotating a ski outward on a U-shaped uphill you INCREASE the steepness of the uphill rather than decrease it like a herringbone should do! It can be IMPOSSIBLE to herringbone up such hills! Frustrating! But we've discovered a way to do it fast and easy! Hooray! You sidestep up one side of the trough! But it's not regular sidestepping -- you're

not exiting the trough sideways. You're not even stepping sideways! You pivot BOTH ski tips toward the center of the trough and raise BOTH tails up onto the side of the trough as you scamper up the hill! Your skis make a parallel angle going up the hill. The poling action feels somewhat normal but has a sidedness to it. One hand reaches farther up than the other. Keep your hands as low and normal as possible. Try it! It's fun to keep it smooth and relaxed. Don't lift your skis any more than you have to. Keep them low. You're lifting yourself enough, I'm sure!

Down, Down, Down!

To just glide down hills get in the ready stance. To get comfy on downhills, practice shuffling from foot to foot while gliding down. Move from side to side across the trail as you glide down. Now practice stepping and shuffling your feet around a downhill corner.

Remember, to get into our ready-stance, just jump up and try to land without making a sound: this gives a nice deep flex and puts your hands in front. Feel free to stop at the top of a downhill and do this jump to get ready.

Our method for control on downhills is the same as with alpine skiing: hands "on steering wheel" in front of you, in boxer or wrestler position, or lower. Shins pressed forward -- to get control with alpine skis we press shins into the front of our boots -- that weights the tips and lets them bite and work to keep us safe. In the end, make sure your feet are evenly weighted from heel to toe. Stay out of the "back seat" -- if your weight goes back onto your heels even a little bit your hands will start to rise up and reach out -- you become unstable, get stressed, and risk crashing.

Once you feel stable, get in a track and try to rest on a downhill. It's easy to glide in a set track. It's a safe place where your skis won't go in any strange new direction. They're like a railroad track. Tuck your poles under your arms. Drop down. Try a few postures to see how they feel and how they might be good for you: hinge from the waist with straight legs resting. Or, drop torso to thighs to get into an aero egg shape. Keep your hands together in front.

If you're nervous about downhills, or a hill in particular, get yourself down it slowly somehow first. Snowplow, sidestep or even take off your skis and walk down. Then from the bottom walk up a ways and try to glide down part of the hill. (You can walk up and put your skis back on from a sidehill stance or you can herringbone or sidestep up the hill.) Go higher and higher up the hill until you reach your limit for downhill comfort. Taking a downhill one part at a time is a good way to learn how to ski the whole thing. (I use this method myself when trying to sort out a technical downhill on a tricky trail that I want to do again better someday.) Of course some hills may always be too much! There is always a way to handle a hill. It doesn't always involve skiing the whole thing!

With singletrack trails not designed for skiing, as soon as you have any significant downhills, you need "black diamond" level descending skills. What I've described are standard scouting practices used when kayaking a new whitewater river or in any adventure skiing. Be careful! Build up.

For groomed trails a track will be set for all manageable downhills and their related corners, but once likely speeds are high enough for a given radius of corners the tracksetter will be raised and the course left smooth for skiers to handle as they may, usually by way of snow-plowing.

You can keep your skis in groomed tracks around corners up to quite high speeds for maximum glide. It helps to flex ankles and knees and get lower and lower in your tuck. Then to get around a curve over-rotate your tuck to keep your skis in the tracks: move your hands far to the inside and turn your torso far to the inside as well. You can stay "glued" in the tracks while still going very fast, before you need to step out with one or both skis, or opt for some amount of snowplow braking.

Some fast down-hills will require an

alpine ski racing trick. If they have a rise and drop in the middle of the downhill you will want to do a pre-jump by jumping before the rise and pulling your feet up under you so that the "lump" in the downhill doesn't throw you.

Braking and Stopping!

Yeah, skis don't have brakes. Skis are more like a fixed-gear bike: direct drive – your only brakes are your feet. So, to brake you'll snowplow with each ski -- weight one ski, unweight the other, move it out to the side a bit and forward a bit, step the heel out farther so that the ski is angled, then set an edge, put some weight on it, and skid the ski. Try one foot then the other as you go down a hill. One foot can be left in a track, if it's a groomed trail. Then try both feet at once. Play with the amounts of edging and weighting, and how far to the side and forward you set the ski. Go between light and tiny snowplows and extreme skid-braking. Notice how a snowplow can also help you turn. You can use the snowplow to stay in control on fast downhill turns by braking with the outside foot.

You can also do a hockey stop. Unweight a ski and set it out in a snowplow, weight it and start skidding, then lift your other, rear ski and set it parallel alongside the first ski and weight it also, edging it away from where you're going. Hockey stop. You can also unweight both skis at the same time by dropping down then extending your legs then pivoting both skis together and setting them both on edge. Total instant hockey stop.

Hit the Deck!

Sometime you'll misjudge a hill or make a mistake or just have life happen to you. Don't worry. Snow is softer and slidier than dirt. But still be careful! If you're going to crash or just want to bail out on a downhill, sit back on your tails and slide down on your butt on top of your ski tails. You will still slide but more slowly. You can also just flop back to the side on a butt cheek then put your skis below you and across the trail then stand up and side step or snowplow down the hill. Don't let yourself go down a hill faster than you can control your skis! It's better to bail out early than to wait until you're going too fast. Try to always fling your pole baskets behind you as you crash. Both skis and poles do a good job of getting out of our way when we tumble because they're only held onto us by one pivoting point that moves quite freely. Ski gear is so light that even when it's torqued it doesn't tend to overburden our joints so injuries are rare, unlike in alpine skiing where the gear is so heavy and the skis are attached to our whole foot, creating huge lever forces which severely injure a huge percent of enthusiasts.

Well, you've probably been at it a good hour by now. ...Time for another swig and snack!

Then maybe call it a day and see if your brain can stop swirling.

Skilz: What's Up with Skate Skiing? —"what you learn will shock you!"

If you want to skate-ski, start by both reviewing and doing what I teach in the chapter on Classic stride skiing. Most of the fundamentals apply. No skipping!

I also note that just as with the Classic that I am not completist. I'm giving you an overall view of the skills. And the photos I'll provide don't cover everything. I'll also post a video to my YouTube channel to show what I mean.

I've been studying skate-skiing from when it started, all through its development.

My goal is for learners to have fun every step of the way -- no wasted motion or time, no awkward drills. Indeed, I use the fewest drills possible.

Skate skiing is fun and fast on prepared courses with the proper gear. It's no harder than regular classic skiing. Don't think it's "harder" or that you have to be "fitter." Don't be a struggling ski-waddler. Here's the fun way to do it. Check it out!

My big point about skating is that it's no more or less work than stride skiing. I often hear and read about skating that it's "a lot more work!" It's not.

It's true that skating today tends to be done by a fitness-oriented demographic, but this isn't necessary at all. Casual skiers can have fun skate-skiing, too!

The main thing is that skating isn't done on a narrow or soft, ung-roomed trail. It doesn't have a singletrack Trail Skiing aspect and isn't commonly done in a touring mode, although it easily could be as long as the trail is wide enough.

Sometimes a walking trail works for skating! Here I am in low snow, in a light rain, on a park trail. Fun! Amid all the vintage gear I'm using, I'd note that low boots are fine for short skate outings.

Skate-skiing usually needs a groomed or otherwise wide-packed trail about 6-8 feet wide. Snowmobile trails can work quite well for skating, though probably only a smallish fraction of them are wide enough and smooth enough. Quite a few places groom their snowmobile trails (thanks to the funds that agencies get from their licensing). So if you catch them at the right time, some popular trails can be smooth! It's important to only ski on snowmobile trails during off-hours that see low machine use.

Well-designed skate-ski trails can be a thrilling rollercoaster ride. However, often

their wider width means they are in mellower terrain than nearby singletrack.

Firm, fast crust is awesome for skating. Frozen waterways with a crust can be great. But when the crust is "on" when the terrain is at least somewhat wide-open, then skating is a blast over hill'n'dale with no grooming needed.

You can go on long skate outings. You could skate all day on crust, or a long snowmobile-type trail. You could skate with a loaded pulk and camp out. Casual skate touring and adventure skating could become more of a thing. Tim Kelley in Alaska does a lot of this and has a book and website dedicated to it.

The Speed of Skating

Skate-skiing has a mystique of speed, strain and difficulty. (Conversely, skate-skiers can be intimidated by classic skiing and consider its technique and waxing to be "too hard.")

In fact, the leg and arm actions and posture of classic ski-striding and ski-skating are the same -- just with skating the kick is to the side -- that's the only difference! The thing with striding is that to get power the foot stops for an instant, grips, and you leap forward off of the stopped foot. With skating the foot never stops gliding. And that's why it's a faster style. But as you become more skilled the speeds of the two modes get closer together.

If people don't have a good understanding of both modes it is easy to misunderstand either one. This is only a problem if it keeps people from having as much fun as they could. Like, if people think skating is the "fun" way and so only have skate-gear -- even when only one flat little local golf course is groomed for skating and there are dozens of singletrack trails around. Or, conversely there might be awesome skating but only a few striding options -- though this is far less common, since literally everywhere is good for striding while skating has limitations. They both are awesome when it's right!

All skate gear is basically race gear, and it's done in fast conditions, so this is the first-order level of why it's faster than touring on ungroomed trails would usually be. Any kind of skiing done in skate conditions would tend to be fast.

Also, on singletrack, skating isn't fast or fun at all -- because you can't hardly even do it! (Sometimes people can squeak out some skating fun if a trail is packed only 4-5 feet wide.) In such cases, striding would usually be faster.

Remember, you can do skating at any effort level you like. But like with any skiing, if you don't know what you're doing you'll waste energy and work more than you need to. This is where skating gets its reputation of taking more effort.

Partially, I'm writing this -- and making videos -- because the other info I see out there, including the official methodology, is race oriented. It shows skate-skiers in lycra bodysuits and elite physiques. It often uses fancy medical terminology. "Extension through the obliques!" ...C'mon! Anybody can do it, for any reason. You don't need no steenking tech-nerd-geekery. I'm guessing that 90% of the folks who could be having fun with ski skating won't be racers or elites. However, the sport has introverted itself enough that mostly only "Type A's on Overdrive" seem to be skating, but I'd rather see us bringing in, um, everybody. Coz it's fun. It's like rollerblading. No need to get fancy, tricky or complicated.

As regards skating being "a lot faster," for beginners it really can be. For intermediates it's about 25% faster. For experts it's only about 10% faster. For long events, it can even out: I just saw World Cup results where a famous marathon time recently was faster for classic than for many years when they skate the same course.

But just by waddling along, as a beginner, maybe even with no instruction, you can move swiftly on the flats with skating. Wheeee! It's harder to zip along with classic striding skis using just the uninformed ski-walk method. Waddling is faster than walking! But with instruction both modes become HUGELY easier. Classic increases more in efficiency with instruction. With skating the payoffs come more up front, and can be had on flat terrain even without instruction, but instruction helps hugely with it as well.

In short, skating is faster because it lets you put out more power. How? Its power-phase is longer and the power portion also includes glide! With striding the ski has to STOP each time! And when Classic skis aren't stopping -- as when doublepoling -- they aren't powering. Yet skating loses some efficiency because the power is going SIDEWAYS quite a bit. Skating can use more muscle with each stroke but its overall tempo is slower. The net effect, though, is a gain. ...However, when uphills get steep enough that the skis start to point much more to the sides then Classic can suddenly compare quite a bit more favorably -- and an Expert strider can pass an Intermediate skater. ...Physics is cool!

Is Skating Harder?

Since the power-phase of skating is longer for both legs and arms it uses more muscle, but since it's a slower tempo it uses less aerobics.

Skating is like riding a bike that's always in a bigger gear. With classic you're spinning. You can go hard or easy both ways but you're always using a bit more muscle in a bigger gear.

So you can dial skating to whatever effort you like. One kind of skiing isn't harder than another. It's up to us!

The common mistake with skating is that you can go pretty fast on the flats even with bad technique. You can pile on work when you don't have to and waste your effort. It's like the difference between a big young new swimmer and a highly skilled old-timer: the newbie thrashes to exhaustion while the old-timer relaxes and glides.

In ski-skating it's easy to "get in the back seat." You can still waddle-ski like this and have fun on the flats but it's TWICE as much work! On uphills it's even harder. That's why people say that skating requires more fitness or takes more work.

The Differences with Skating

A huge benefit of skating is that waxing is simpler since there's no kickwax or grip to worry about. Ever.

You glidewax the whole base of your skis. And the skis are about 8" or 20cm shorter than striding skis. This is for maneuverability and also because there's no gripzone taking up acreage in the middle of the base. Fit is based on your weight and trail firmness or softness.

Skating poles are about 10cm longer than striding because they're set out at an angle from the body and they plant a bit further back so that a ski can be pushed to side while the poles are planted. Also, skating is a double-poling technique, which puts more bodyweight on the poles. Lastly, since it has a longer power-phase it has a slower tempo so we can use longer poles without bogging down.

The boots are stiff everywhere except for flexing the ankle forward. This is because you push to the sides and power comes first from the heel then the whole foot before a toe-off.

You can fudge shorter poles, etc., for a little while just to get a feel for skating, or in a pinch when out striding. And you can get by with touring boots. And even classic length skis can be OK for a short jaunt. But you really don't want kickwax or fishscales.

The Names and the Moves

Skating has 5 moves or "gears" to help you go up the steepest hills the easiest (lowest gear) or to zoom down a gradual downhill the fastest (biggest gear). Just 3 of the gears will do you fine as you're learning. Indeed, many good citizen racers and funsy skiers mostly use just ONE kind of ski-skating. It's called the "V1" and you can do a lot with it and play with it and change it around. (It's called other names in other countries. "Offset" in Canada and "Paddling" in Norwegian, "Hoeing" in Finnish.)

I think part of the problem with the lack of popularity in skiing in the USA is our branding: the names for our ski moves. Well, some might be good, but others have issues. What would be better? Maybe someone with marketing savvy could help?

Let's start from low gear for climbing the steepest hills to our biggest, fastest gear.

Diagonal Skate: First gear. This is for the steepest uphills. It's like the herringbone stride in classic only the feet keep moving. You pole with one arm for each opposite skate.

V1: Second gear. The most versatile and useful of all skate moves! The tech-

nique for climbing most hills, but easily adapted to also work on the flats or slight uphills. Restful and stable. (We were so relieved when this move was invented! We could finally climb fast and easy!) It's not intuitive but is readily taught and then one very naturally senses how to modify it for all uses. Quite a few skaters use this move nearly all the time. This move has a strong-side and weak-side. You doublepole and skate off of the "strong" foot onto the "weak" foot. Then you skate off of your that weak foot (which is "weak" because it has no poling-assist) while swinging your arms back forward again. You land on your strong foot, then start poling and skating off of it. The poles are held asymmetrically with the strong-side pole held upright and close to your head and the weak-side pole planted further back and to the side and so the polehand starts lower and in front of the shoulder. It's a great move for uphills because the poling and a skate happen simultaneously. Both feet should often work equally but sometimes the strong-side foot takes a bigger step and kicks harder. On uphills you quickly skate off of the weak-side to get back to the power. You don't change the direction of your torso much on a steep uphill. Instead you keep your feet moving. But for the flats you can hang out a bit on the weak-side to enjoy some glide. There it's sometimes called "ride-and-glide." It can also function more like marathon skating. Indeed, it can segue into marathoning if you have a usable track next to you. (It's called Offset in Canada because the poling is offset from the skating.)

Marathon: The first-ever skate-skiing move invented. Rarely used, but worth mentioning. Use it when it works or is fun. Sometimes your skis are gliding best in the track and it's OK to skate from the track without anyone getting mad at you for marking up the track. This move started the battle between skaters and striders because it was done in and across the tracks and chews them up. It's best on the flats or fast conditions or slight downhills. It's a scootering move for skiing on a trail that is groomed for both striding and skating and the stride tracks next to the skate-lane are already messed up, yet you can still get some tracking guidance from what remains. You put one ski in the classic ski track next to the skating lane then simultaneously doublepole and skate, starting with the tail of the ski of the skating foot crossing the tail of the gliding ski that is down in the track. You unweight the gliding ski a bit as you skate. Don't ever skate across a doubleset classic trail. It isn't officially placed as a "gear" in the series.

V2: Third gear. Doublepoling with every skate action. For working while you skate and for slight uphills. It's for conditions that have some friction so you add poling power to each dose of kicking power. You doublepole and at the same time skate with, say, your left foot over to your right foot. Then you rise up and doublepole and skate off of your right foot over to your left. Rise up and doublepole and skate back to the right. This move requires more balance than the others, but with the right equipment and a few tricks it's easy to do and relaxing. (In Canada it's called the One-Skate, since you skate once for each poling. In Norway it's Dobbeldans, "Double Dance." Some folks say "Gear 3.")

V2-Alternate: Fourth gear. Umm, this is our weakest name. Sometimes said "V2A." Or, Open Field. (Help?) You skate evenly with your legs while doublepoling with every other skate. It is so fast that you only want to pole half the time. This move is for fast conditions, often on the flats. Start by poling and skating on one side, say the left, then over to the right side where you just glide with both of your arms flung back. Now whip your arms up again while skating again from the right foot back over to the left. Then doublepole downward and skate off the left again. It's a natural, intuitive technique. People will often figure out its basics on their own, but it has subtleties that help make it fly. The sport relied on it for a couple years before inventing V1. This move tends to bog down on uphills. (In Canada it's called Two-Skate, since you skate twice for each poling. "Gear 4" in some places.)

Freeskate: Fifth gear. This is skating down a slight grade without using any poling. You go like a speedskater and maybe swing each of your arms back and forth in front of you or from side to side as you skate. You're going too fast to use the poles.

Learn a Lot Just Standing there!

Time for dryland motions. No skis, poles or snow needed!

Swing your arms together and then separated, fore and aft, 45 degrees bent, let em fling, relaxed, lead with front of hand, make a motion like tossing cup of water down trail in front of you.

To practice skating leg action, stand with legs shoulder-width apart then shift hips to the side, over one foot so that the other foot lifts off the ground. Back'n'forth. Each foot lifting off in turn. Now shift hip over and down, flexing knee and ankle a fair bit, letting other foot lift up, then stand up and shift to other side and do the same, going up and down on the same foot. In a kind of upside-down U motion. Now let's try a different leg/hip action: Stand on one foot, flex, lower your hip, then shift to the other foot, stand up, lower, then shift to other foot. In a kind of regular U-shape motion. So, that's a couple different ways you're going to achieve the needed weight transfer, and leg action for propulsion.

Add some *umph* and hop from side to side. Not too far. Whatever feels OK. It can be very light and small. Try to land in balance on the other foot and let your off-leg float up like an outrigger. You don't have to freeze anywhere. Good leg action in skating is a push to the SIDE only. With your whole foot. Push from the heel, then toe-off. Gliding happens more when you stand up on a ski. Powering happens when you flex deeper in knee/ankle and give a shove to the side.

More Background

Skate-skiing is a lot like ice skating or inline skating. But many people do those kinds of skating wrong. And it's not like figure-skating! And it's not like the running-action in hockey skating. In short: there's no toe-off to the rear. You don't step or kick BACK. It's more like speed-skating -- they push to the side only.

Skating is easy and fun for many people because there's no worry about kickwax or getting grip on uphills. And there's no stop-part to coordinate. Gliding happens all the time. Even if you're casual or sloppy there's still gliding!

The problem of stride-skiing is there's less tolerance for messing-up. If your butt is back in skating, you just work harder, but you can still get around and you can still get up hills even though it's a ton of work. If you don't stand up on your skis in striding then you can't get grip to ski up hills and you'll suffer.

In skating if you don't push to the side "early," with your weight over the kicking ski, you can "wash out" the tips of your skate-skis quite easily and waste effort. This happens when people kick late because they're floundering "in the middle" and out of balance. By not being relaxed as you move from ski to ski in good timing you also waste effort. Also, if you're herky-jerky you can shove harder than you need to with each leg or you can strain awkwardly with the longer poles. So skating can seem "hard" -- even though it isn't! However, to get the greater speed you are putting in more work. And it's paying off more! So you'll say "it's faster but more work." But you can dial-back on skating to whatever effort you like. Really, one kind of skiing isn't harder than another. It's up to us!

The key to skate-skiing is the same as speed-skating: there is no static part of the motion. You constantly and relaxedly are moving through each cycle. There's a "pulse" of harder effort, with a fast kick and a lingering glide, but you never freeze up. That leads to stalling out and you just have to re-accelerate. Your body might not be literally over the ski, but you kick right down onto each ski for your whole kick. You press your knee and shin down toward the front of the ski.

A big error is "bailing out" of the move. It feels easier to "fall off" a ski than to kick down then move over in control to the other ski. But falling off wastes energy. It happens when a skier is rushed and out of balance.

Time for Arm-action in Dryland

Let's now add arm action to our dryland imitations to complete the various skate moves. We can easily do them all on dry land, just stepping around in a room or outside, with no gear. In fact for one of the moves doing it on dryland is the easiest way to master it on snow.

Yes, these are drills. They can feel like no-fun and not-skiing. We're itching to get on snow and have the fun! . . . Patience. It won't take long and they get you ready for the real thing.

One thing to practice as you go through your dryland imitation a few times is just stepping from side to side not forward. In fact, a proper skating kick shoves forward with the heel weighted and pressed down as long as possible. So doing it best on dryland means moving BACKWARD. But we won't be that extreme.

This should be a great time to look at some YouTubes. However, at this time I can't find any that show basic dryland imitation (quite a few fitness drills, though). I'll make one and have it posted to my Outyourbackdoor channel on YouTube by the time you read this. Really!

I'll list from slowest to fastest:

Diagonal Skate: (1st gear) Easy. Step back and forth raising the opposite hand in front of your shoulder then swinging it down as you step. Flex your knee downward just before you step over, straighten as you step.

V1: (2nd gear) Stand centered over your right foot with your left toe a few inches to the rear and touching out to the side just beyond being below your left shoulder. Bend your right leg a bit and flex the right ankle. You're poised over that right foot. Bend your right arm and raise your right hand up near your head about shoulder height. Bend your left arm and raise it about as high as your lower rib-cage below your left shoulder. Now pretend to do a doublepole and step or pivot over to your left foot. Your arms are now extended down and somewhat to the rear and your body is centered over your left foot (with bent left knee and ankle) and your right toe is touching the ground. Now step or shift back to the right. You don't need to lift your feet to do this. But raise your hands back to the first position as you shift back to the right. So it's hands up on the right, shift to the left while moving the hands down. In this description the right side is the strong-side. The move should be able to be done equally on both sides, but people sometimes have "handedness" and prefer a side. The V1 action is described as "3-1-3-1-3-1 …" It's helpful to say it aloud. The "3" means that on the strong-side you set the ski and plant the poles at the same time. You kind of fall onto the poles and ski simultaneously. 3 things hit the ground at once. Then you power all 3. The powering sends you over to the weak-side where you sometimes glide a bit. You can hang out longer or shorter on the weak-side depending on the speed of the terrain or the grade of the climb. The "1" is when you skate off the weak-side ski while whipping your hands upward. (Note that a quick up-motion with hands helps the weak leg kick down a bit harder.)

   Marathon: There is no great benefit to doing dryland imitation for this move since it's about scootering, but you could put one foot next to the other, angle it out, then step over to it then step off of it as you raise and bend then lower and straighten your arms.

   V2: (3rd gear): Dryland HUGELY helps you learn, get a feel for, and improve this technique! In fact, dryland is a must. So let's see what words can do. Stand up with a slight forward tilt from your ankle and centered on your right foot with both arms raised and bent with your hands in front of but near your head above your shoulders at ear-height. Your left toe touches the ground off to the side a few inches beyond your left shoulder and a couple inches behind the right foot. Now pole down and bend your right knee and step over to your left foot. Now your right toe is touching the ground and you are centered over your left foot, arms back. Raise your hands up above your shoulders next to your ears. Now pole down, bend your left knee and shift over to the right. That's it. Do that a few times. Now get bouncy and jump from foot to foot while doing the hand-action. Let the off foot come off the ground several inches and hang there an instant then swing over and "gather up" under your right hip near the strong-side so you can focus all your weight there then it swings back as you jump back over to it. You could let your two feet click together in that "gathering" phase as you're poling and flexing the skate-side leg. Are you wobbly when you try to add a hop? If so I find that minimizing hand/arm action helps, as does less torso motion. (This is one move where you don't whip your arms upward fast in recovery. You lift them gently. You're gliding during the arm-lift, not doing any kind of kick, so a fast lift doesn't help.) Turn the poling into "flicking." And just keep a stable torso tilt going with a little crunch-compression. Also, hopping over to a straight glide-leg, letting your leg-bones give restful structure to the pose, can help. Having the off-leg and finished arms all floating out to the sides acts like balancing poles for a tightrope walker.

   V2-Alternate: (4th gear) Imitation doesn't hurt, but dryland isn't known to benefit known weakpoints in this technique. Stand on your right foot with your hands in the air. Pole down, compress your torso down a fair bit (more than with V2) then after you're nearly done poling, jump over to the left foot. Arms down. Jump back over to the right foot, starting with your arms down and whipping them up. Finish raising your arms once on your right foot. Forceful arm-whip gives reactive power to the weak-side skate-off. The finished arms act as balancers for gliding on the weak-side. Enjoy the hang-time. The faster the conditions, the longer the hang-time. Repeat.

Freeskate: (5th gear) Imitate for grins. Doing so doesn't help any known weak-point. The arms swing side to side in front of you as you step from foot to foot. Or you can tuck your imaginary poles under your arms then step from foot to foot.

Almost Ready to Skate-ski!

To get ready for skating we go through all the same familiarization drills that we use for Classic, with the following exception:

To skate we step onto a FLAT ski to glide then we TILT or EDGE that ski to the inside to get even bite all along it and step/push/kick off of it to the other side. We kick off an edged ski. And we glide on a flat ski. Our skis smoothly roll from being placed down flat to rolling onto their edge as we kick. What's cool, tho, is that they're gliding all the time! ...But they glide most when riding flat on the snow. And to glide nice and flat we need to have all our weight on a ski. To kick off an edged ski we will flex our knee and ankle more than they already are and push and put MORE than our bodyweight onto that ski to propel us down the trail.

Skate-skiing! ...Well, HALF of it!

Find a flat place and take your poles off and set them aside. Let's ski without poles. Point your skis in a 40-deg Vee and rock back and forth from one foot to the other with your knees/ankles flexing, pressing your knee and shin down toward an area about a foot in front of your binding, pushing to the side, straightening and gently let the ski float off the snow to the side. You should be moving! Quite easily. Add arm swings to the sides to help you with the rocking. Opposite arm and leg. Moving more! Now add more of a bounce to your leg flex. Moving even more! There's some glide now! Now swing your arms fore and aft in time with your legs. Opposite timing just as if you were walking or running.

As you can get more power and glide more, you might start "washing out" the front of your ski. This means you're pushing with your toe. It also means you're pushing too late: you're stepping over to the other ski partially THEN pushing, so there's less weight on the push-ski when you push and it washes out. To fix that, visualize pressing each push-knee down to the area of the ski in front of the binding. Push when your weight is centered over the ski then step over to the other ski. Don't "fall off" one ski to the other.

Try to recoil off of one foot and get a good glide onto the other foot -- and stand up momentarily on that gliding foot and put your off-hand up to your brow and pretend to "scout" and look off to the horizon. This will inspire you to a longer glide and a more upright posture when you're gliding.

Skate from side to side and give a hop on each foot once you're over onto it. This also teaches you to stand up on the gliding ski.

Try to skate up a slight hill -- swing your arms and bounce from side-to-side and compare swinging arms fore and aft and side to side.

We're Skate-Skiing!

FINALLY! ...Put poles on! Do it right -- hand up thru, then grab down onto strap and pole.

Skate poles should be as tall as your chin or nose (or between) when you're not on your skis. But really you can skate a little with any poles on any skis! (If you're using waxable striding skis try to scrape off the kickwax first so you don't have needless grip in the midsection. Nowax skis will work a LITTLE bit for skating, but not really.) Real skate boots also are good because they resist bending at the toe, helping you push with your whole foot and supporting your foot while you do so.

Skate around using your poles. Use a pole action just like how you walk or run. One pole on one side at a time, opposite from your foot-push. This pole action is the same as for stride skiing. This is your lowest skate-gear. You can go up a steep hill doing this. It's called the "Diagonal Skate."

To pole, use the same basics as for Classic poling…

That is, to repeat: Plant the basket near your feet, maybe a bit behind them. With skating because your feet are sometimes splayed, staggered or spread apart more

than in Classic, our poles are longer. That's so we can keep them out of the way of our skis and feet.

Your hands should be in front of you, close to you, with your arms bent about 90degrees when they plant. When you push you'll drop your weight onto the poles in a 'crunch' action and you'll push your hands at your baskets until your hands are just past your hips.

It's OK if your hands are more in front of you or out to your sides but in those cases they are being used more like outriggers, for balance more than propulsion. Whenever you push down on a handle and the basket is right below that handle your force is only support, no propulsion. Your poles only help you move if the baskets are planted BEHIND the grips/hands -- if they are angled to the rear and if your hands are somewhat close to your body. If your arms have a good bend in them then your upper body, back and torso-weight can help you pole. If you just use your arms you will be much weaker and get tired much more quickly.

You can practice poling on a flat or slight downhill using only your upper body and not your arms by getting into a track and holding your arms fully bent and tight against your body. Now just make little rocking crunches of your torso. Drop your knees a bit for power then stand up to recover. You can pole along pretty well like this, not using any arm action at all.

It's good to tilt forward a bit as you plant your poles and to "fall onto" your pole-straps. That gives good power and helps with good posture. To do this, try to deepen your ankle bend and slightly increase your knee flex. Do not bend more at your waist.

STOP FOR A SQUIRT OF APPLE JUICE AND A SNACK!!!

V1: Now for Real Skate-skiing!

Now we will learn to apply the most versatile skate move: the V1. (It's called other things in other countries. Canadians say "offset.").

It's about the only ski-skate move you need. You can go fast with it. You can 'gear down' with it and go up a steep hill. And anything in between.

I've already described its features and I've shown how you can become familiar with its basic feel on dryland anywhere. Now I'll lay out how it goes on the snow.

This move has a power-side and a glide-side. But there is glide and power on both sides. One just often gets a little more than the other. You can play with it and vary it to what you like.

In V1 we doublepole AND kick at the same time off of one side onto the other side. On the other side we can rest a bit, or not, as needed or liked, but all we do is just skate off of this "weak side" or "off side" and fall back onto the "strong side" for another simultaneous pole and kick. Now… The strongside pole and kick don't happen exactly at the same time nor do they each last as long but they START all at once. We fall onto BOTH poles and the ski at the same time.

To change the "gearing" of this move all we do is change the angle of the vee of the skis and the timing of the kicking.

The faster we go the more we glide on the power-ski and the more we delay kicking on the power-ski. We can also change how long we glide on the offside.

Going up a steep hill, we vee out our skis a lot and use our poles and kick immediately to combine all our forces to give us a nice "low" gear for easy hill-climbing.

For going fast on a flat, we delay our kicking until after our poling to stretch out the power and give us a "bigger" gear for more speed and less leverage.

So! To further ingrain how to do the V1 we take our poles and skis off again. We step from side to side flinging our arms in a doublepole motion on one side and not on the other. We move in a pattern like "3" and "1".…2 poles falling down and 1 foot (3) pushing off of one side then just stepping to the other side and raising the arms again getting ready to fall/step back over to the other side. 3 1 3 1 3 1. It usually takes SEEING this on a video or in person to "get it." But give it a try!

As you learn V1 you might sense that you can use a TWISTING motion as you pole from the strongside to the weakside. We do like our body and weight to go from ski to ski but we want to keep ourselves pointing DOWN THE TRAIL rather than pointing from one side to the other with our shoulders or hips. To tell if your bodyweight is in the right place your knee and even your nose might be right over the top of your each ski. But face down the trail.

Up We Go!

So, to skate up hills, just shorten up both your poling and your kicking. Try light flicky moves — on the flats, then also on the uphills.

Here's a tip to get a better feel for skating up a hill, and to find a posture that saves your energy: splay your skis in a vee at the bottom of the hill, pointing up the hill, drop your butt then tilt forward at your ankles, then rock from ski to ski, now add your V1 poling motion to assist then add more leg action.

The steeper the uphill the more vee-splay you'll have but still keep your motions light and short and keep your chest pointed up the hill and pole with both hands shoving back down the hill. Press your shin toward the top of each ski.

The steeper the uphill or the slower you're going the more your V1 hands will be offset, with one hand high and the other lower.

Breathe "deep deep easy easy" -- let hanging from the poles help you let your belly sag and let your poling help you to 'woof' exhale.

(STOP FOR A SQUIRT OF APPLE JUICE AND A SNACK!)

The faster you're going and the flatter is the terrain the later you'll kick after poling. And the more your skis will point down the trail rather than to the sides. You'll be able to enjoy "ride-and-glide." You'll fall onto a flat ski in the "3" mode, pole, then delay some with your weak leg just kinda dangling under you and your power leg kinda straight under you, too, relaxed, then it will flex and kick over to the weakside where you'll land on a flat ski and just hang there as well on kind of a straight leg with your power leg kind of hanging as you rocket along. This is called "bone on bone" skiing, where you have a naturally balanced phase on each ski that doesn't use much muscle or tension in either leg and where the offleg just hangs for a moment.

STOP FOR A SQUIRT OF APPLE JUICE AND A SNACK!!!

The Full Enchilada — V2 & V2A

Once again, here are the 5 gears of ski-skating: Diagonal skate > V1 > V2 > V2A > Freeskate.

We've already gotten a feel for V1.

V2 and V2A have different poling patterns and other nuance differences compared to V1. They're fun and not too hard. They are somewhat faster moves than the V1 -- meaning, you use them when you're already going faster than with V1. No technique "gives" you anything for free. Lots of skiers just use the V1 and play with that move to go faster or slower without needing any V2 or V2A at all. So you won't be missing out, especially early on, if you skip them -- though, of course, like all skiing, they are fun!

For V2 you want to be able to do it nice and relaxed on dryland before trying it with skis on snow.

It's important to note that for V2 you really want ultralight carbon poles! They make it a lot easier.

V2 requires more balance: but it's not

static balance. It's learning to, at first, reduce the range of some motions to optimize your dynamic balance. That is, don't fling your arms or legs much. That way, it's easier to balance.

Really, with all ski moves you're never "trying" to balance. If you are, it's wrong. "Trying" sounds like straining and seems unpleasant to me. Why not just "do" instead. Don't forget: all skiing is fun, even the learning! So when a move needs more balance do what gives balance. The balancing comes from doing it right, at the right time, with the right gear.

When V2 goes wrong, people often find themselves tipping over to the outside, or bogging down, or speeding up in tempo uncontrollably as they rush each move a little quicker to catch themselves and stay balanced. But none of these problems mean that V2 is "harder." Or that it "takes more work." You just need some help.

If you tip to the outside, try stepping a little wider from side to side. We tend to get lazy and step down too soon, before we're done pushing off the other foot so our momentum tips us outward -- be sure to get that foot out far enough to be under you when your push is done. Or, think about weighting your big toe so that your weight doesn't get out toward your little toe on your foot. If you find yourself waddling and falling back to the inside then visualize weighting your little toe more, or don't step out as far. Do a little more dryland side-hopping til you can do it very relaxed, even with your eyes shut. Little things can help a lot.

If you bog down and feel like you're exerting hard with each poling, just don't

follow-thru as much on the poling -- use a light 'tap' to keep the tempo up yet without working too much.

So start with short, small, light moves when learning, especially with V2. Avoid too much torso action: V2 doesn't use much anyway.

Remember: grandmas can do all-out moves, relaxed, at what seem like slow speeds… until they pass you. So, figure 'em out for going slow then use 'em for going fast.

There's a dictum in cyclocross that "slow is smooth is fast." Skiers can use it, too!

V2-Alternate is quite easy and fun because it uses the most arm-flinging and "biggest" motions yet feels natural and stable on both sides of the stroke. You may well naturally fall into it on faster, somewhat downhill sections. Optimizing it takes more work, though, including this key detail: to get more speed from your weak-side skate-off whip your arms upward forcefully. The harder you whip them up the more force gets applied downward to your kick – your arms can help your legs. It's also fun getting comfortable with the hang-time aspects of this move, especially when your arms are done poling and they fly out like outriggers.

We've already done the no-poles Freeskate when we were first learning to skate. But now you could try it down a hill to go as fast as you can! Your poles are still on, but you fling your hands from side to side, holding the pole baskets out to the sides. If it's crowded or you're going too fast for that, tuck them under your arms. Then after that's too much, just tuck and glide!

Down, Down, Down! (Skating)

Dealing with the technical and high-speed cornering aspects of downhilling when skating is easier than with comparable classic gear. That's because skate gear is all relatively of a race-grade performance level. Race-grade classic gear offers less support and control, still we use all the same basic skills when descending with skate gear. Skating boots and skis offer very nice cornering control and edging power, enough to throw parallel turns with confidence. Enjoy!

Mixing It Up

Out in the real world of skate-skiing you might mostly be doing V1. It's easy to adapt to both climbing and fast-flying on the flats. But after you become confident you'll start stringing together the several different techniques as you ski through varied terrain. This is where the big fun comes in. It's a blast to groove some V1 then throw in V2 for awhile then switch to some poppin' V2A. Changing it up through the transitions lets you keep your flow mojo rolling at a peak.

Skilz: Basic Backcountry Concepts

Backcountry skills have two main features that run along a continuum: trails and turns.

At its lightest, BC means skiing ungroomed trails. Then it moves up to beefier MTXC "mt-bike of skis" gear for skiing challenging singletrack (which is usually ungroomed but now with snowbiking is sometimes groomed). Then the gear gets wider and stronger yet and we start throwing in linked telemark turns as we cruise along. Finally our heaviest gear lets us enter a world of turns in every kind of snow followed by uptracks back up to do it over and over again.

To party in these scenes you really should do 3 things: Take a telemark class. Yeah, they're hard to find, but do it. Then watch YouTubes. Then read.

I'm not going to give a how-to, just this idea of progression and the big picture concepts plus a variety of tips. Some of this will be for never-ever's, other parts might come in handy for experienced skiers who are new to BC.

BC is its own book-length subject. I know 3 titles in print. They're all great and the first two I list are short and full of cartoons! "Allen & Mike's Really Cool Telemark Tips" and "Allen & Mike's Really Cool Backcountry Ski Book" and Paul Parker's "Free-Heel Skiing."

Singletrack skills are presently untaught in the official arena. I do what I can here and in the rest of this book, and in my videos at my Outyourbackdoor channel on YouTube.

First Tele

First, find a firm-packed, smooth, gentle downslope, like part of a kids' sled-hill, that you can learn and practice on. You could also get a lift ticket at a local ski hill.

Start at the beginning and go through the standard progression of Green > Blue > Black. That is, from Beginner > Intermediate > Expert. And be comfortable and confident with each degree of slope before moving to the next.

Once you know how to alpine ski or snowboard or even telemark ski at a lift-served resort, you're ready to learn BC skills. If you're used to skiing moguls with alpine gear, turning on light XC skis will be similar but different. So take it stepwise.

It bears repeating again and again that once you start skiing singletrack trails that weren't designed for skiing if they have

Here a hardwoods glade run on a tidied-up backyard slope anchors a mile loop that features a neighborhood ridge combo platter of singletrack, glades, brushy technical trail requiring slalom turns, and open fields. 70mm BC skis and light leather BC boots make it a thrill-fest of striding and turning, but a really wide range of gear can all be fun.

much technical descending involved they require a black diamond skill level. Be careful! Get to know your trail slowly before trying it faster. Try half a hill before you try a whole one. Trail skiing is a new sport in the USA! Even if you're a Nordic racer or telemark skier, you'll need to acquire new skills to safely ski hiking and mt-biking trails and other routes that weren't designed for skiing. So, scout your lines like an elite whitewater kayaker or adventure skier.

As with all downhill ski learning, go up it only as far as you're comfortable coming back down. A little at a time is fine. If you find yourself too far up, it's wonderful how easy it is to get out of your modern bindings and walk down to wherever you feel safe to start. Or sideslip down.

Don't go on a group tour of technical BC

terrain or singletrack while you're learning. You need to avoid the tendency to try to keep up, so you can freely repeat anything as you like.

The main three things about descending singletrack are the narrowness of your available route, and the variety of moves you might have to make in quick succession, and your reduced opportunity for soft bail-outs. Problems with any of these limiters will mean hazard.

To begin, when descending, drop a few inches lower, flex your ankles, keep your hands low and in front of you.

If it's a straight run with a clear, easy run-out you can tuck and get aero for top speed if you like, or you can stand up more, but still stay in the ready position.

Groomed tracks give you security, but lack of tracks gives you options.

Out on your packed sled hill, work on hockey stops and snowplowing for both braking and turning. Also practice stepping from side to side -- comfort with fancy footwork is essential. Singletrack can surprise you with roots and rocks in the trail, mixed with descending and turning. Being comfortable with stepping back and forth as you descend is key.

If a narrow downhill trail is too steep and fast for your comfort, first try to find slower snow. If possible, step one or both skis out of the tracks and into the deepest unbroken snow available. Due to unevenness and narrowness, a snowplow might be hard, but you can often do a few quick mini-snowplow bursts of braking to scrub speed. If you're dropping down a gully or along a sidehill, try to side-slip or skid on the uphill slope with your tails pointing to the trail. The challenge is to time your moves around unevennesses and obstacles.

To change which ski is weighted and skidding, suddenly rise up a bit then drop again, changing your ski position as you stop rising and unweight. Weighting and unweighting are the keys to moving XC skis where you want them to go. XC skis, bindings and boots aren't strong enough to cheat and do this by force. Indeed, no skis like to be pushed around. The unpredictable nature of BC snow and obstacles makes this even trickier. Quick weighting and unweighting lets you choose places to make control moves.

You can thread your way through a lot of singletrack by managing different kinds of skids and snowplows.

Also, feel free to drag your poles as you go, but don't let your hands drift back. Don't stand up high or lose bend in your knees and ankles. You can even take your poles off and hold them both upslope as a drag.

If you get going too fast anyway: sit down and to the side sooner rather than later, unless you know you have a safe run-out.

If you don't know or like the looks of a downhill, don't start it. Don't follow someone else unless you're confident. (Especially don't follow RadNord.) Ski within your own skills at all times. Look to the

sides. Check the lay of the land. There will be other ways to get where you need to go. Traversing is your friend. Leave the trail. Pick a line as gentle as you like and glide down the side-slope, stepping or turning back uphill whenever you come across something you're unsure of. To turn to ski the other sideslope direction, depending on the slope steepness, you can make a downhill step wedge turn to get yourself pointed onto the new traverse, or you can stop and swing your tips up and around herringbone-style to prevent gravity from having its way with you.

Now, if you would like to link some turns downhill, you'll have to weight and unweight your skis sharply. Strongly standing up then dropping, moving the skis into a new snowplow or parallel skid when you're unweighted.

Now we get into two aspects of ski skill which open the doors to the rhythm of

What goes down… Heading back up the uptrack to do it again. This particular uptrack is adjacent to the glade run pictured on the left. You can watch skiers going down as you truck up. The uptrack is also a place to chat with pals about the last run.

Down again: Descending with Marquette Backcountry Skis in their steep, brushy element. These snowshoe-skis are made for quick scampering up and shredding down ravine-like settings.

descending.

These are the basics of linked turn rhythm. They're easiest to learn on a smooth slope. Then you can gradually step up to the BC.

Keeping your chest facing down the fall-line lets you link turns. Angulation lets your skis work to carve, ski, skid or plane while your chest is pointing down. That is, your chest is pointing downhill, your hands are low and forward and your skis are pointing to the side and your knees are deeply flexed down. For maximum speed braking control, your skis can point completely across the slope even while your chest points downhill. Your knees will tilt into the slope to make your skis "bite."

Practice swinging snowplow turns down a well-packed gentle slope, feeling how your skis behave as they turn while your chest faces downhill. You can reinforce your skidding downhill ski after you make a snowplow turn by letting the uphill ski drop down alongside it and tilt its uphill edge into the slope as well. This is putting you on your way to doing parallel turns.

Then you can take the next step in your progression by planting your downhill pole, stand up (or even hop) then while you're dropping, turn your skis entirely the opposite direction a few feet further downhill from where you were. If you would like to glide some while this is happening, you can leave your skis on the slope as you turn. You can also turn them less angled across the slope. The more straight they point the faster you'll go. The more you tilt them into the slope and turn them across the slope, the slower you'll go.

Look ahead, especially in tree skiing, to be able to enjoy a rhythm. And don't look at obstacles: only look where you DO want to go. If you have a spill and find yourself a bit nervous and start looking in dismay at what you're facing, take a break. Shake your head. Look at the snow, not the hazard. You will go where you look!

Narrow XC skis don't have much edging power, especially when they don't have metal edges. So as a slope becomes steeper you can find yourself wishing for more control. You can get it by using a telemark turn. In the telemark as you weight your skis you drop your hips and flex your downhill knee and pressure your big toe (first micro-hint) then tuck your uphill foot back under your butt and flex that knee and snug it behind and into your downhill knee and weight your little toe (second and last micro-hint). The telemark turn in effect gives you one longer, curving ski rather than two short ones. XC skis also flex a lot. The front ski curves at the front and the rear ski curves to support it. Keep your hands low and in front.

The original telemarkers over 100 years ago used a single long ski pole staff called a "lurk." Using such a pole (or sapling) is being done again today. It's fun! When both hands grip a staff to help you change directions, neither hand can drift up or back. A lurk forces your both of hands to stay in front of you, a wonderful encouragement.

The fun part is the rising and falling and the changing of your feet as they cross the fall-line in front of your chest, again and again.

Changing the angle of your edging and the degree to which the skis angle across the fall-line will determine the speed you descend.

The width of your trail will determine how much you have to edge and how quickly you need to weight and unweight. For the narrowest and steepest of runs it's reasonable to jump-turn down a slope, not letting the skis glide at all between turns.

The condition of the snow will also affect how you handle your skis and the amount of resistance it'll put up to your smooth progress.

The main thing determining your fun will be the continuity of your rhythm.

Up again: A singletrack uphill is very different from a simple zig-zag uptrack. It's often less than straightforward. Which is a good thing! It's satisfying when you can keep the flow going.

...Then we press on and soon ski down similar pitches.

Quick lateral footwork makes technical climbing and descending relaxed and interesting rather than stressful.

Fascinatingly, trees are easy to ski in and around. Snow is also held best where trees are. Just don't look at them. Don't think this: it's what you'll do without thinking. Just ski the snow.

In powder skiing you ski from your core, your belly button. You can't focus on your gear in particular. There is no "edging" because there is no firm bottom. In general skiing with light gear is always like this, which is why it's fun. The gear is not giving you the power and control. It's the overall rhythm and control you establish as a sum total of each tool you have. No one item gives very much support, but they add up to enough.

When first learning, one can benefit from unwaxed skis that glide slow. However, once you catch on, waxing your backcountry skis will let you make the most of gentle slopes. And sometimes you'll want to doublepole from a flat over the brink to gain speed before starting a series of turns.

You can have as much fun as a person can handle, skiing over hill and dale.

Ski Party: A Spring-Fever Epic

A Cornucopia of Cornography

Hardcore cornography. That's this year's Jordan Jam.

Actually, it's almost always like that.

It's a session of intense ski-swimming.

Skis swim, doncha know.

Skiing the corny backcountry of the Jam is kinda like powder skiing only it's over all the terrain, not just downhill. You kick and glide, climb and descend, but not against anything firm. You constantly monitor your center of gravity. Your skis porpoise up to the top now and then when you lean back. A soft tip is good. A little rocker in a BC ski might be good, too. Right now only pure tele boards are rockered. It's time to give more love to all-round BC gear.

But corn... Corn is poetry. Of course, like all good things it's nearly entirely ignored by The World. Corn is snow that has thawed and frozen a few times. The crystals become big, round and juicy. They sparkle in the sun. And they can take the heat. Corn is strong. On sunny, warm, late winter days it can be 50 degrees in the corn and your skis are still lovin' it. It's not sticky. As long as it freezes at night corn can last for weeks.

Skiing has two seasons, ya know: Winter and spring. Skiing isn't just about the fluffy cold; it's also about the warm corn.

Our group's skis were all very different from each other. They varied in type, style and width but they all worked great in the foot-deep corn. It feels "bottomless" but you DO get some nice control, performance and kick'n'glide!

The Jordan Jam is a wonderful grand finale. It's our springtime sayonara to the ski season.

And it's a tear-jerker. It's hard to let go. Maybe we should taper out our season instead of ending it with a bang. Because after each JJ I don't want to quit. (Up north people get another month!)

Speed isn't the thing at the JJ. It's about wallowing in the experience. Literally.

The JJ is the last of our six-part Michigan Backcountry Ski Series. We ski the Jordan River Pathway in the NW corner of the Lower Peninsula. It's a bowl of watersheds that drop down off a big plateau, a 19-mile loop with 4000 feet of climbing. It's technically a hiking trail. Mt-bikes aren't allowed (I don't know how much summer pres-

sure the trail gets). And the literature says "Highly NOT Recommended for Skiing." Switchbacks, trees, steep descents ... with no run-outs -- that's why the warning.

But we ski it anyway. We find, with the deep snow, that we can readily detour into the forest to scrub speed.

It takes us from 5-10 hours, depending. ...That's a LOT of depending!

It's a comical day for us down-staters in terms of the RadNord pace of life. (Rad-Nord is a local ski hero and dangerous person. Don't believe him when he says "it'll be easy."

RadNord drives the paddywagon to pick us up at 5am, drive north 4 hrs, ski all day, have a beer, then drive home by 10pm. Talk about roadbuzz!

We start and end at Deadman's Hill. This finale of the tour is a one-mile super-steep climb back up from the valley to the high plateau. ...It's gorgeous.

This year we started in near-freezing weather under clouds. Perfect. The snow was a good foot deep. Corned up but not

scarily crusted.

Six of us set out, including three (expert) newbies. Rad, Dick, Dan, Marcus, Reinhold, and me.

Reinhold showed up out of the blue. He heard about it then came. That's how it works. Few are called. Fewer answer.

Our preferred daypack set-up might be said to be a narrow backpack plus a fannypack, since the fanny can be rotated around to the front for easy access, but other variations can work fine.

We were all enjoying our rigs. Nobody was suffering -- nobody going off the front.

Well, Dick always goes off the front over the early ridges. He has a beautiful, lively style for such an ancient person — even on Rossi BC 90s and 75mm bindings!

He also knows some good Bob Dylan lyrics. As our merry band marches along we sing songs, often making up our own lyrics. But some lyrics are so good there's no improving on them. This kind of outing is a time for enjoying such things.

It might've been neat to all use the same bindings so we could've each used the widest skis as we took turns breaking trail.

Our patented all-day method is: after 10 minutes of trail-breaking the leader steps aside and drops to the back which is now nicely tracked-in and easy, perfect skiing.

This mode of BC travel has everything in the world to recommend it. I assume every BC tour group uses it. It deserves its own movie, but how much press has it gotten? Well, we've made sweet YouTubes about our fun. And now here's this book! It's a start!

The skiing at the front is work. Sometimes stunning, even numbing, in its intensity. Well, we're fit for a reason, right?

Dropping back you're greeted with the bliss of kick'n'glide. And recovery. As you rotate forward your work level gradually increases.

With this method your experience changes, your ability to observe the world shifts into the background as the burden increases. It's a delight of nuance.

What's more, it's inclusive, don't you see? Skiers of different desires and fitness levels can work together seamlessly. Those who are relentless can do longer and more frequent pulls, in a futile attempt to burn off energy and fever. (Sometimes the sounds of pretend motors hardly fades during the day. *Brrrap brraap! Vrrroom vrrroooom!*) If you get tired, or need to fuss with something you can stay at the back more and enjoy the half-energy needed to go twice-as-easy. It's a delight. Some might take fewer pulls. No worries. They help pack the trail! We all do our part. We're a team.

So, we chugged along at a modest pace yet it was still an athletic achievement. We might herringbone for a quarter mile at a time, sweat pouring down onto the snow in front of our spraddled legs. On downhills we revel in a greater variety of techniques.

The JJ has it all. ...The views, the little scenes as you swing around the outer prow of a contour, or go winding up a valley. ...The snacking. ...The basking at the main bridge over the Jordan River. ...The

sound of all the brooks we ski along as we encounter different watersheds all flowing down, down, with the melt.

I like how the Adventure Skiing System is of a piece. It's not a question of which wax is working, but more how does the whole thing work. If any part isn't optimized the whole thing can fail. ...Ski, binding, boot, pole, pack, gloves, camera, food, drink, brain.

Don't forget your repair and emergency gear. (A spare binding is smart. And 5-min epoxy. One of us once needed to wait for a beeler ride out after pulling out a binding.)

The trail crosses over a half dozen ridges then drops into as many deep creek watersheds, changing from hardwoods up top to cedars and hemlocks down by the

varying waters. A delight! It's a watery, watery day. We saw otter slides and a messy coyote deer kill.

The sun came out now and then as our day warmed. Then the snowpack quickly became unstable. We floundered in mashed taters. Then, whew, we'd swing around the contour and find some shade. A flurry of wintry mix came and went.

"Wintry mix" – Michigan's new swear-word. No, we can dig it. It's all good! …It's a combination of snow, sleet and rain.

We crossed the Jordan itself twice. Flowing water in winter is so beautiful. We don't get to see it much downstate, though it's there if you look. Even when we ski on our local river when it's frozen there will be occasional open places with flowing water -- which I always love to see. …. With all the wild animal sign that such places attract.

It's a delight to smell the water in the air. Spring is in the air. Vegetation, earth and growing things are again part of the scent.

We all wipe out a few times -- but these last chances to lay in glittery, juicy snow are more a time to laugh than complain.

Occasionally on exposed southern slopes we tramp through brief snowless areas where pine needles are damp but being baked by the sun. That smells great, too.

Every hour we'd stop for a snack. These are snacks to relish. I should've brought white wine, even a little whisky. Heck, where was my dried fish and cheese? We savor our snacks, but we stick mostly to pizza. I'll remember more variety next time. It's an aspect too important to shirk in the haste of getting ready. This is an outing to savor.

As we skied RadNord enjoyed dictating a little blurb into his phone then using his Songify app to turn it into a cosmic ditty on par with Mr. Double Rainbow Across the Sky.

We had a little joke that stuck in some of our heads. I suppose this happens with every group. And probably you had to be there. I had noticed a day earlier in front of the Lansing court-house a sign that says "No Freestyle." Had lawyers been getting too loose? Was there a problem

with judges not following precedent? Of course, under the sign it said "no skates, bikes or boards." After I told what I saw, we adopted the concept for our skiing. Whenever one of us did something goofy we'd holler "Watch it with that freestylin'!" Or on a tricky descent someone might say "I don't care about the rules, it's time for a little freestyle." … The things that people think are funny when they're sweating for hours.

We elected to skip a distant section of trail when we finally got to it, in favor of a snowmobile trail, for the variety mostly. We are not completists. We enjoyed a mile of easy skating along old farmland with its rows of derelict old maples along a snowed-over dirt road.

If we'd skied the entire trail we would've climbed all 4000 feet. *Whoa.* We've done it before. This year we climb 2600 feet. One year it was perfect corn over crust and it only took a little longer than it takes to ski the Potto, our other favorite singletrack -- which has four times less climbing! It was a big skateboard park with herringbone.

For the day's grand finale we also missed Deadman's Hill because of bridgework blocking our route. Instead we enjoyed the detour of a steady mile skiing up a snowmobile trail at a shallower incline. We were kicking the stride and gliding the glide the whole way. Great glide, great kick — up, up, up.

Otherwise that day whenever we had climbed it was herringbone. Probably a mile of it. I love herringbone. Skiers sometimes talk bad about herringbone. It's a technique where they check out, or just waddle. It's not really skiing, right? Wrong. A couple hours of herringbone will cure you. Relax. Enjoy.

If you can't get enough herringbone, the JJ is for you. …Ski you next year.

So Much Tasty Gear...

You're pretty well set up to handle gear. You have google to answer questions. Then make friends with the folks at the nearest shop that sells XC. If there's nothing local, find a nifty online shop and give them a call. They'll be happy to help.

The big snag is I doubt anyone knows about our radical new "mt-bike of skis" MTXC concept. But if you explain it they'll catch on. ...Ski gear for singletrack shredding, adjusted narrower or wider to suit the other ski angles you want to include.

So I'll just hit the highlights...

20 Innovations...

Oh, the awesome improvements we have enjoyed in ski gear in recent years!

And in addition to ski gear, we find developments such as: hydration packs, the revival of wool, multitools, digital devices, and ultralight gear of all kinds. (I still think it would be neat if we brought back the Bota Bag – the ubiquitous wine sack that was so popular in the hippie days, when skiing was a party not a workout.)

But let's focus on ski gear. Here's my list, by casual rank. I went quite far back since these items will be new to most people (because we're dealing with a blank slate in terms of public awareness of XC). If you want to know more, just google!

I think this line-up could be promoted right now to the general outdoor sports world, for the first time, to deliver a fresh boost to the sport.

Maybe you'll find it refreshing as well...

1* Modern NNN, BC, and SNS Bindings. They give so much control!

2* Modern Skis. Today's cap skis let designers control flex and handling characteristics better than ever.

3* Carbon Poles. Once you get gungho, carbon is king. Mid-grade models are light, strong and affordable -- very similar to top-shelf.

4* Striding Boots with Pivot Cuffs. They give wonderful control and support for singletrack skiing.

5* Midlength Skis. With the new cuff boots and BC bindings, these create the mt-bike of skis. Easy to handle on singletrack, they come in many flavors, mostly nowax. Narrower for technical speed. Wider let's you link BC tele turns. Metal-edge models for max control. Often (mis)labeled as "intro" skis.

My quiver has skis to cover all the conditions I encounter ... BAM! And it sure is pretty. I keep skis as long as they last since they fill specific functions. The main thing is being able to ski all the kinds of snow. Overall investment in this awesome mish-mash of vintage gear is about like 2-3 pairs of new race skis.

The MTXC "mt-bike of skis" set-up. ...Midlength midwidth skis, modern bindings, sport poles, boots with pivot-cuff. Let's us ski our favorite snow-country singletrack with confidence. For intense terrain, use more width, metal edges, and a BC binding.

6* Wide BC Nowax Skis. From 80mm wide up to 125mm with rocker, these fat, shaped touring skis with fishscales open up the backcountry to miles of kick'n'glide plus steep powder turns and surfing over shrubbery.

7* Light BC Boots. From the Rossi X6 BC "tour boot on steroids" to light plastic boots like the Garmont Excursion, these give you power for BC turns yet are nice for striding all day.

8* Adjustable BC Poles. They started out flexy, club-like, and unreliable. Now they're great. Boost fun for BC turns.

9* Tele Bindings. NTN, Hammerheads and Bulldogs are the cool modern tele bindings -- potent, and some of them release. But a 3-pin with cable is still a light, awesome, cheap rig for a lighter set-up. The populous hardwoods seem like the sweet spot for tele -- especially since AT has pulled ahead in the mountains.

10* Fluoro Waxes. ...Coz they so fast. (And rillers and brushes. Also fast!)

11* Cuffed Pole-straps with easy click in/out. So nice on your hand joints if you ski a lot.

12* Groovy Waxes of So Many Flavors. It's a blast to HIT THE WAX right. Kickwax, klister, glide, supplements: it's a crazy scene that gives great results.

13* Pattern-less Nowax skis. Rubberized "hairy" grip sections and fuzzy "skin" grip sections are setting free nowax skis from the buzzy fishscales. They grip and glide better than ever, especially in the dread "zero" range around freezing, which is ever more common with climate change. The concepts are trickling down to touring skis. (Replaceable gripzones, too?)

14*Steel Scraping for Glide! A Russian scientist discovered that a super-sharp steel scraper makes a base smooth enough to give good glide without wax. Not for racing, but still. Scraper only lasts a few sessions and is pricey.

15* Grip Tape. This stuff rocks. It started as a way to simplify waxing with one tape working great all the time, but now has added its own temperature ranges, giving me a scare.

16*Best Concept in the Wings? "Move" bindings are new and cool because they let you easily move them on the ski, to give more glide or more grip. Even wilder would be a button on a pole-grip to auto-move the bindings. Add them to skin skis and Kuzmin glide-scraping and

What Gear is Right for You?

How to decide, out of the rainbow of ski gear on the market today, what to buy?

This is a rabbit hole I'm not going down, except to give you the big picture.

I suggest getting real human help.

First, think about how you're most likely to be skiing.

Also, consider who you might be skiing with. If there's a local gang you'd like to hang with, you're almost good to go. They'll likely have gear you can borrow and try, and someone to show you the basics and point you in the right directions.

Then find your nearest ski shop. (Tell them who sent ya.)

If there isn't a shop with a decent variety of gear nearby then look online for a place you like the looks of. They're all good. Call 'em up, say Hi, and then...

Tell your new ski pro pal about yourself and how and where you picture yourself skiing. They will then set you up.

It's not hard! You can also google to your heart's content.

The goal isn't to get you any particular scene. It's to match you with who and where you are.

Nowadays, skis are fit by your weight. And by trail conditions. And by the type of

maybe we can ditch wax altogether!

17*Best Snowsport Innovation? ...Snowbikes!

18*For the Best Ski Feel? ...Full-length classic skis and kickwax. Yeah, it's an old combo, but it has yet to be surpassed for so much skiing.

19*A Big Need? ...A US XC ski company or even label!

20*An Even Bigger Need? ...Public education and PR for XC and winter fun!

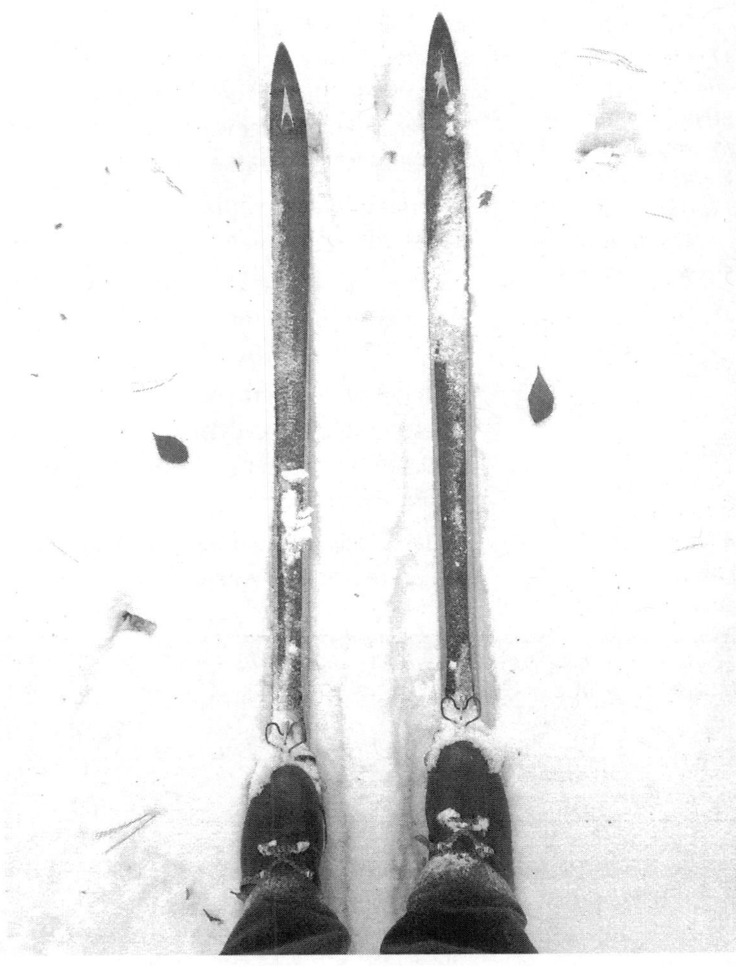

Woodies can still be awesome in cold, soft conditions.

This high-end combi/pursuit boot gives awesome control for singletrack skiing. Cuff for support. Flexible forefoot for easy striding. (Also OK for skating.)

desired action.

Older classic touring skis were fit by your height, in addition to style and conditions.

All gear today is pretty good quality.

Skis

Ski traits are fairly intuitive...

The wider the ski the more turning power and float over varied terrain. Narrower is faster on packed trails.

Stiffer skis are for firmer conditions. Softer skis for squishier snow.

The longer the ski the faster the glide. The shorter the ski the quicker the handling.

Modern mid-length no-wax skis are awesome and the cat's meow for singletrack fun. Pick a beefier model for more technical terrain.

Classic skis have a double camber -- an arched center area where the traction-stuff goes. You press it down and it grips. Traditional flex fitting for casual skis is done using the "paper test": when you stood on both skis on a flat surface you should be able to slide a sheet of paper a foot or so in front of your toes and a few inches behind your heels. All your weight on one foot should pin the paper.

Length-fit for traditional striders is they go to your raised wrist, more or less.

Skate skis have a single camber (no grip to worry about) and are basically flexed so they are flattened at 90% of your weight. This is checked with a compression gauge clamp. You can use the paper test creatively for approximate guidance. Length is usually about 2-5" taller than you.

For new skis, all brands have online charts.

Poles

Any pole will do for casual outings. But the more you get into skiing and the more fun you want to have, the lighter and stiffer your poles should be. Poles make a huge difference, exactly like paddles do for boaters.

Sizing is to armpits for casual fun, to shoulders for sport. Adjust from there based on druthers and terrain: hills like shorter, flats like longer. (Skating goes to your upper lip, but it too varies a bit from that based on style and terrain.)

Carbon is a great material. Thankfully, you can get a mid-range pole that is hard to distinguish from a top-shelf model for about half the price. These poles

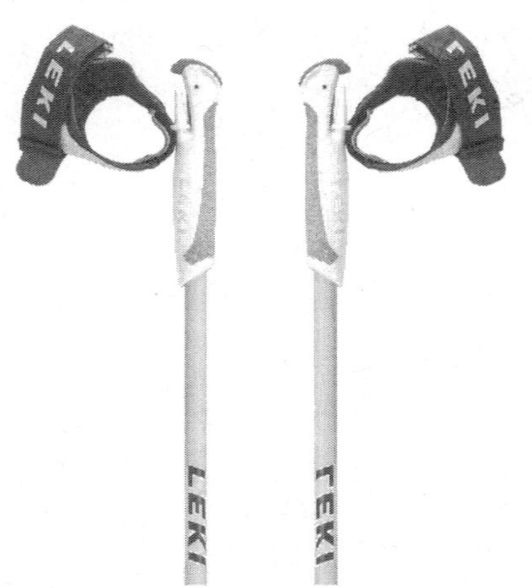

don't like sharp impacts, but otherwise they're tough as heck. I crash plenty and have had mine for decades. I guess I just know how to get the poles out of the way as I go splat.

Today's sport poles mostly come with tiny baskets suitable only for hard-packed or groomed trails. If you ski singletrack, consider replacing tiny baskets with 2.5" models from infinity. They're the only maker I know who offers performance baskets for diverse conditions ($18 pr).

If you ski a lot, today's cuff straps are easier on your hands.

Boots

Modern boots are awesome. Your ski pro will set you up, whether at a shop or online.

The coolest recent innovation, as per my list, is the pivot-cuff classic boot. The nicer the boot, the nicer the cuff. Again, opt for beefier for more challenging terrain.

For fit, you want a snug heel for classic. And you want a snug forefoot for skate.

Bindings

Today's bindings are so good! They make ski handling a breeze compared to back-in-the-day. We needed track-setting because without grooves our skis had a mind of their own! Soft, low boots plus 3-pins or old SNS-1 bindings only gave hints of surf-board-like control (still great fun).

Modern NNN and SNS are all sweet. Automatics allow easy step-in, click-out. However, check them for sloppy play! For best control opt for manual bindings: they hold the boots the tightest. (SNS-Pilot, with its double-retention, seems good only for groomed hard-pack skating. Icing is an issue, especially in ungroomed striding.)

Left to right: 75mm 3-pin, old SNS-1, older NNN-2, racing NNN-2 for NIS plate, SNS-Profil, SNS-Pilot.

Binding tech might become quite cool in the next few years! It's a case where tech complexity might really boost the sport -- though I could be getting overly excited. The concept of changing gears like on a bike might be coming to XC! That, plus further reducing the role of fussy wax! Here's hoping.

Food, Drink, & Picnic!

Skiing isn't the only thing that's great about skiing. Food tastes so much better when you're active outside!

So, in addition to ski gear you're going to want to have a few more things if you start getting into fun skiing and trail action. Because you'll probably start going out for a few hours at a time with your pals.

Racer and fitness types in lots of kinds of outdoor sport eat and drink while they're out there, but it's bars, goos, gels and chemical potions. Yeah, I'm sure that after trying a few you can find some that help you and agree with your stomach and wallet. But some of us are encouraging folks to eat real food. You're a nicer person when you do. Sure, include some of the high-tech stuff, but also bring a picnic and share it. This means you'll need a rucksack of some kind. Here is what we've learned…

First, for the food, once you start skiing real trails you're going to be going up and down more than usual, and turning with more force and mental focus. You'll work more. And you may well find you need to tone it down a notch below your groomed golf course intensity level if you're going to enjoy a full loop of skiing your favorite singletrack. Also, your gang will be having so much fun that you'll want to be out there a few hours. This all points to you eating Real Food. All the more when it is cold out. Yes, there will

be weeks when it's in the teens or colder. As you chug along you'll need to keep the homefires burning.

We have found that an ideal food is PIZZA. Indeed, a slice of deluxe cheese and meat pizza seems suitable for skiing an hour or two. So that we gauge our outings by the number of slices they require. A four-slicer is basically all day. Pizza has the fat and protein that keeps a body happy, warm and energized when chugging along accomplishing challenging tasks for hours in the cold. We discovered this little-known fact after repeatedly bonking when trying to fuel such efforts with only carbohydrate-based bars, goos, gels and potions. Keeping up on your electrolytes is also a good idea. As is the occasional caffeinated item.

Stopping for a group chat at a best vista deserves a true picnic spread. Find a sunny log to sit on. Pull a jacket or vest from your pack. Change your hat. If you get sweaty feet or hands, change your socks or gloves, too. Bring along something to sit on. Maybe even a square of ensolite foam pad, or just an empty part of your pack.

…And haul out the oranges, nuts, stinky cheese, crackers, cured meat, and chocolate. The Bota Bag of white wine comes in handy now to squirt streams of chilled nectar from. Everyone dig in! Everything tastes better in the cold sunlight after you've been skiing. No, it tastes GREAT. But it helps if it's great to begin with! (Apple juice is nice, too. I remember seeing apple juice in clear plastic cups on a table in the middle of the first ski race I did when I was 20. It was a 20k and I was in over my head. It was sunny. I'd just crossed a bridge

over a crystal clear creek and stopped and stared at the sparkling water. Then I saw the sparkling apple juice. It tasted great. …It has ever since. Maybe you'll like it too in the middle of a nice fun sunny ski day.)

Apres' Ski Parking Lot Party

Parties in the parking lot will become more of a thing if XC catches on again.

Most times after a long, hard work-out ski groomed trail skiers will just disperse back to their data-caves.

In a world where homestyle XC skiing is popular you'll have socializing. And good food and hanging out. Plan to stick

You don't need a lodge to have an awesome apres' ski experience. We're lucky to have wild game chef Dave. Here he's whipped up venison chili and his own tortilla chips in the parking lot for our gang of a couple dozen fun-hogs after a 2-hour outing.

around. But make sure you're comfy!

You're likely done skiing, so change your clothes into heavy, dry, warm gear. Put on a heavy coat and heavy boots. Outside of springtime fests at a few resorts, we're not used to tailgating in our ski culture in the US. You don't want to get chilled. Get dry. And, unless it's actually warm sunny springtime, get well-insulated.

Your vehicles can haul everything you desire for a cook-out and bonfire. We tailgate and bring chairs, firewood, grills, a bonfire fire-pan if suitable (salvaged small car hood). Use a battery inverter to run a hot-pot. And, whattaya know, summer coolers keep well-wrapped hot food hot for hours in the winter. Guy out a tarp between vehicles or trees for a wind-break. RV's qualify.

Snacks for casual half-day ski outing. Mmmmm, pasty. Wide range of snack-groups represented to help keep the zest zesty. Note the combo of rucksack (red) and fannypack (black). Fannypack rides under rucksack and is easily rotated to the front while on the trail so you can get at snacks, map, phone, wax, bevs...

Packs for Everything...

Here is another aspect of gear that, as with clothing, you can have a lot of fun with, or you can just opt for a common tech item. Consider that you might have this pack in your life for decades. Why not look for one that you actually think is cool? Sure, they're functional. But they can also be tasteful, fashionable according to your ideas. You could get a waxed canvas pack with leather trim that you can wear til it's burnished and hand it down to your kids. Whatever pack you get you can customize it, add patches to it. It's yours. Why not own it?

It's like bikers who go riding without a bag on their bike: where's their spares kit? What if they wanted something? Sure, going "naked" works for a quick workout near the house, but really having fun often means more than heart-rate. Packs, bags and pouches are part of skiing!

First, skiers need a long narrow pack that fits snugly in the middle of your back and doesn't sway.

Then there are the different sizes of packs. Even for a casual jaunt after work you really might want to have a place to stash your outer shell or your thicker hat once you warm up. It doesn't have to be big or heavy, just a little something that works. That you like. Heck, fannypacks and even deep zippered vest pockets can be essential for bringing little must-haves. They are all worth being thoughtful about. Then you might have a bigger pack for longer outings. For longer-yet, combine pack with fannypack. You might even end up with yet another pack big enough for overnights or weekends. Packs are a thing. They can be key to our fun from shortest to longest adventure.

Hydration packs seem to have an ideal shape. (Foam insulation wrapped around any exposed sipping tube is good, or just keep it tucked inside your shirt.) Our packs usually don't have to haul all that much stuff. We aren't typically like loaded backpackers. We need to stay dyno.

We use the size of pack that has room for some clothes in the main pouch in addition to a bladder (if desired). Then the snacks go into a large outer pocket. For longer outings, fannies are cool because you can rotate them to the front to get at stuff you need while on the go, without taking off your rucksack.

(Mindshift Gear is a brand of rucksack that contains its own rotatable lower portion that you can swing around to the front. It looks awesome but I haven't tried it.)

Make sure that your hands and arms can easily swing fore and aft without bumping into any part of your pack or make anything sway from side to side. Pouches on the front-side of shoulderstraps seem like they could be handy. Beware of hipbelt side pouches or front pouches – poling and dropping down with your torso have to both be unencumbered.

What's good to have in a fanny pack? Snacks, map, kickwax, camera-phone, a different beverage than what is coming out of your sippy-tube.

I find that a 15-pound pack, overall, including food and drink, is the most I want to carry for a day-trip. And I always start skiing with such a load for short jaunts for a couple weeks before attempting an outing where I'll want to enjoy carrying it all day. A pack really increases the up-and-down work we do with our torso while skiing. It adds to low-back tensions as well. We often revise our technique to a more upright posture to make it easier. Skiing is weight-bearing, after all, unless you're pulling a sled. ...It sure is nice as the food and drink diminish toward zero near the end of a big day or longer outing.

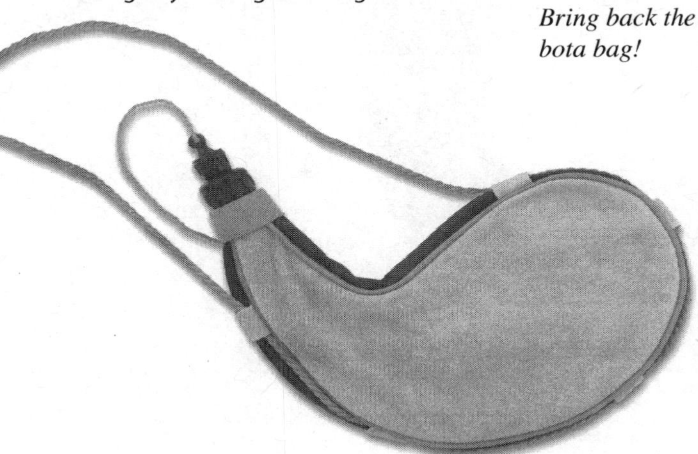

Bring back the bota bag!

Clothing... (Hint: *Wooool*)

I have to say: the best active winterwear is wool. Fine weaves don't itch.

Test whatever you're thinking of wearing and make sure it helps make your winter experience perfect. You should not put up with any discomfort whatsoever. There is no reason to say "Brrrrr!" in winter. You should be warm and dry no matter what. ...Sure, you might occasionally get to "enjoy" the burn of extremities adapting to

Wool, wool, wool!

bloodflow through what feels like frozen tissue but that's a good thing.

Typically, people are chilly when they start then they warm up. The solution is easy! Wear a few layers. Like a shell then a medium weight then a base. ...And bring that little lightweight pack. As you warm up, shed a layer. Easy!

What's coolest to me about being active in the winter is that I'm never actually cold. Winter is a toasty time of year if you play outside! I'm more often concerned with controlling sweat. But even that's a non-issue mostly since I discovered how much my personal bio-system likes wool.

Wool is king. We wear it around the house and for everything as soon as the season's temps regularly drop below 50degF. That's the magic point for us. Again, everyone is different, but wool is rugged, warm, handles moisture perfectly, is wind resistant to the right degree, looks good and doesn't stink.

One of the worst things about technical fabrics is that they stink. Literally. I can wear them once before they need washing. Wool by contrast can be worn for a few weeks of sweaty work-outs before it gets a smell.

Technical apparel has a nifty stylish lean urban fashion look. I don't rule it out for fashion. But wool usually looks good no matter what. So it wins, too.

Knickers are still cool, though. Cyclists have brought them back, but they used to be king in XC. ...They could be again!

I have never been able to wear any form of Gortex and exert without sweating up. I like windproof gear for windy days but it must breathe.

Wear shell-type pants if you fall a lot: they're easy to brush off. But I would overheat in those unless I was tele-skiing on a deep powder day.

Gloves and hands are interesting to me. I find that lightweight to middling gloves work fine down to about 5degF. However, once it gets cold like that or windy around that temp-point, things can be uncomfortable from time to time. Some friends like a 2-glove combo: light inner, shell outer. They wear both until they've warmed up then shed one. Great idea!

I go through a spectrum of feelings in my hands when I ski in the cold. For about 2 minutes I feel fine then cold sinks in as I'm skiing or doing things when it's 10 degF or colder. Then I'll pull in my fingers or even put them under my armpits for a bit. Or I might keep skiing along, sometimes without poles. Next they might feel a dull ache. A couple minutes later might come stinging. But then, wonderfully, they come around, and they then feel the same as they do in our living room!

Wim Hof is a guy who trains himself and his students (and publishes books and a website) on regulating their body heat internally. I'm sure it works! It's a matter of core heat, of capillary valves opening and shutting, sending blood heat to your core or your extremities depending on where your body thinks it should go. You can learn to control this and to "hack your body."

Nowadays I put a premium on simply getting outside every day. ...Especially every day there's snow. I feel no compunction to change clothes. Certainly if time is short I'd rather be outside than so-called "dressed right." So I often simply go out in whatever I'm wearing. I find that sweat dries. Dress clothes can be washed as easily as sports clothes. Jeans are as good as anything unless you're out for over 2 hours. (Forget "cotton kills.")

Being damp is a bit lame, though. Work on the parts of you that get wet until you find a fix. Gloves can be tricky because many get wet when I even touch snow. Or maybe it's because my hands run hot? Finding gloves that wear well with poling is another challenge. Often I end up sewing and repairing to make them last. Nikwax makes natural-ingredient repellent products for waterproofing gloves.

(The problem isn't winter. It's marketing. Imagine our family's consternation when we go into public buildings in the winter and have to deal with the mass insanity of finding it all to be heated to summertime temps and we have to strip down. We have to wear summerwear to movies in the winter and winterwear to movies in the summer. Such lunacy is used as a selling point. The only way our nation can endure is for this to stop. Immediately. If we all come to suffer hugely from some result of that mentality don't say I – and millions of other sane people -- didn't warn us.)

Now, another indicator to me that something is "off" in the US Nordic world is the clothing lines offered have been mono-style and monochrome for decades. They're all techwear. And they're basically

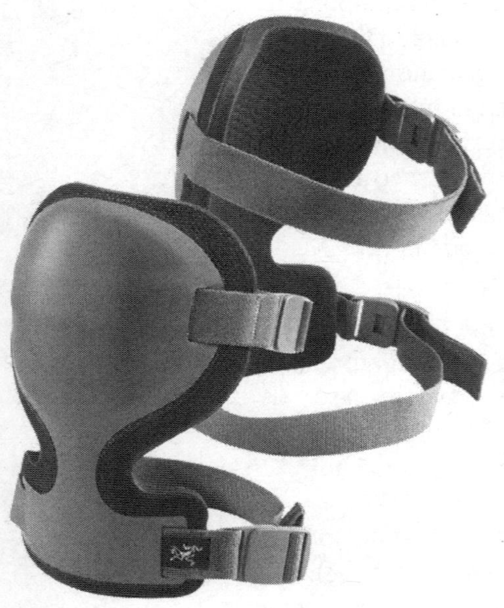

Arcteryx kneepads: thin, light, effective in thin snow and technical terrain.

all black. I've heard that most XC ski-wear sold is black. Thankfully, that might be changing: the latest mail order Nordic shop catalogs suggest ski fashion is brightening a bit. I hope so! Still, when I attend events I notice mostly black. (Except for the lycra, which tends to be wildly garish.)

Snow and sun are the perfect settings for color, fashion, patterns, textures. ...And this used to be the case. I've also heard that as with any outdoor store, most of what is sold is clothes. So to have the best-selling sector focus on a dark urban vibe doesn't seem healthy. I hope they color-up!

We also have lycra, often as one-piece bodysuits. Sure, ski suits are slightly faster for racers. No loose flapping. But aerodynamics are only significant over 20mph. If that's your pace, go for it! Good luck finding a nice-looking one, that isn't garish or chaotic in design. Of course they're also not so flattering on common physiques and can look a bit over-exposed even on those who are ready to model them.

It's odd to me that the suits on the World Cup circuit are colored with little connection to nationalities. The skiers can be indistinguishable in the cacophony of color.

Protection...

Trail skiing brings up a need for impact protection. As usual, everyone is different, as is every trail situation.

If you're skiing fast and close to trees you might want to wear a bike helmet, just like you were mt-biking. If it's not icy and the trail is wide it might be less of a concern.

Everyone in the world of gungho trail skiing has a way they crash. And even gentle skiers can get to know how things go wrong for them. We each have a crash style, our own points of contact where we might fall hard.

Most of us become better at crashing over time, and at distributing impact, rolling a bit, smearing ourselves, sliding into home-plate, so we don't do "pointers."

Deep snow is easy on us. But the thin snow of climate change is much less so. We can hit frozen ground or ice. Sliding is still usually a helpful aspect. But low snow means we're more likely to trip up on sticks, stones and logs -- and then also to hit them when we fall. Thin, junior-level sports padding can be a good idea!

Hands-gripping-poles don't go well with crashes. Thumbs often bear the brunt.

We need to learn to let go of poles when we splat.

We also learn to fall so we don't break our gear. A crash may seem like chaos, but it's not. It's a question of management. We can often flick poles and skis out of harm's way, keeping the leverage of rotation away from them.

But we might notice painful impacts happening to the same places on us when we crash. If this occurs, do something about it. I have friends who get it on their knees. So they wear awesome thin-shell Arcteryx kneecap guards. I have never bumped a knee, but I get it on my hips so I wear mt-bike shorts with thin articulated padding if I'm skiing technical trail when it's icy. I also hit my forearms when it's icy so I have thinly padded football sleeves. Consider inline skaters: they often gear-up. Do the same whenever it fits your needs. Doing tele turns in the trees suggests wearing protection even more so.

Overnighters and Epics. . .

Skiing is highly conducive for using the new generation of ultralight backpacking gear, though there isn't much written about it yet. If packloads can readily be set up under 10 pounds for summer hikes, what is considered sufficient yet ultralight for winter trekking? And how does skiing change this?

UL is a concept where the main components have been redesigned at much lighter weights, often at far greater costs. But travelers have also learned to simplify their expectations and save weight just by doing without.

Skiing will have extra needs in terms of ski care, including wax and repair items. Skiing uses more energy than hiking so more food and water is needed. Skiing sweats more so managing and drying damp clothes is an issue.

A big new trend in biking -- and another fun thing that skiing can learn from -- is the S24O -- the sub 24-hour overnight. This is a KISS version of camping. It could inspire our ski fun. It's not extreme or sweaty. If you'd just like to hang out longer outside now that you're out there, there's now an easy way! Get creative!

All we need is enough stuff to make it comfy for us to head out skiing then set up a camp, get a fire going, enjoy a dinner, then sleep under the stars. Seems like it might be nicer to include daylight at both ends, which can be tricky in the winter when trying to make an outing fit in after work with returning before work the next morning. So set things up to leave early and show up late the next day. Or just do it on the weekend.

The recent popularity of ultramarathons and ultralight gear, might also inspire us. Travelers today might want to do bigger trips carrying less than used to be the norm when skiing was more popular, or even than when it was last written about.

Maybe we want a new ski challenge. We have yet to see a move to multi-day ski events with any noticeable appeal. Snowbiking, though, is thriving in this regard, though, they seem to stick to snowmobile trails and ultramarathons. Not exactly camptime fun, but they're doing it!

I bet we could find some trails to explore that would take longer than a day to do it right.

People love gear. Winter ski overnighting is yet another angle to dial in for gear fun!

Skiers can expect to take advantage of all the new UL gear, such as packs, bags, shelters, pads, cooking, food and hydration gear, and apparel. Still, the weight might be expected to jump up from 10 pounds to more like 30. This seems a bit daunting, offhand, to me. Any tricks out there that we can use? The question when deciding how to haul the load is: Are we still able to safely enjoy the trail we're considering?

Unless the ski scene gets a jump on this, I bet we'll see snowbikers popularizing winter bikepacking before we see a revival of ski camping.

Base Camp with Hub & Spokes

An option that today is viable much less special gear is the hub and spoke base camp: haul your heavy gear into a place that you and your friends would like to ski light orbits around for a few days. Use a pulk to haul out and set up then use a daypack for each day's loop.

The recent "hot tenting" method might be good. Wall-tents and mini woodstoves make good base camps for resting up after daylong loops.

Or just stay in your minivan and use it as your base! Or set up close to where you park. Same as for a parking lot party, a vehicle can easily haul everything a group would like for winter comfort: a big wall tent, chairs, tables, hay bales, wind-break tarps, firewood, chainsaw, fire-pan if desired (salvaged hood from a small vehicle). Heck, an RV would be great, too.

The Pulk!

The option of pulling brings a new player into the equation: the pulk. As with bikepacking, it's smart to let something other than your body carry your gear. A pulk is a sled we pull behind us as we ski. Typically these are connected to a hipbelt by two flexy wands that flex as we ski but are rigid enough to control where the sled goes.

But we need our rig to still be nimble. We want the sled to slide behind us even when going around corners, down hills, or across slopes. One can reasonably buy or make pulks that work great for winter trips and let us ski unencumbered. However, some trails might be too technical for a sled.

An interesting side note is that crossing pulk poles is the best way to keep a pulk tracking straight behind us through corners. Pulks can also be used to pull kids. (I like strapping in an inflated pad chair the sled to give a kid some back support.)

World's Best Sled

Everybody loves sledding. OK, especially kids. Usually kiddy sleds are too nuts, dumb or fragile for adults. My brother and I developed a game-changer of a fun sled. This sled is awesome for the kids *and* for the grownups. Finally, the parents can have as much fun on the sled hill as the kids! (Of course, sometimes you just can't avoid doing some tele'ing on the sled hill while the kids play.) This sled also works as a track-setter and a pulk!

The recipe: Take a common plastic tub sled. Screw waxable XC or alpine skis to the bottom through washers. Glue closed-cell foam into the bottom interior for cushy comfort. Set the ski gap to match a standard XC track-width. Use XC skis for lightness and speed on firm snow. Alpine skis are best for steeper slopes of unbroken snow where you want more flotation.

This sled slides farther, faster, smoother, safer, straighter, and more comfy than any other (that we've seen). Point it where you want to go. There's usually room for two. Add a longer strap to it for easy pulling back up the hill. You can add fittings for pulk poles and tie-downs for a fast gear sled or casual track-setter.

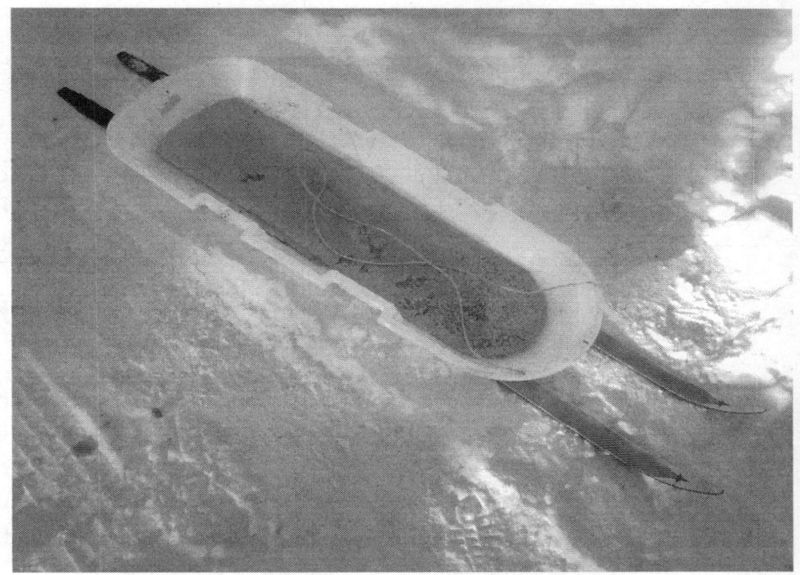

I created shock-absorbing pulk-poles using a 4-ft dowel, eye-hook, bungie and 4-ft metal electrical conduit tubing sized to snugly slide over the dowel. Make two and cross them. Attach to the sides of a padded hip belt. This let me tow our kids (or other load) in the sled while doing stride skiing without constantly re-accelerating the sled. It evened out my workload and didn't jerk our kids heads around. Add camp-pad chair for backrest.

Multimodal: Road Trips & Home Life

Skiing doesn't stand alone. We usually drive to where we ski.

Back in the day, vehicles had ski-racks. We strapped our skis to the roof. Nowadays it seems most skis travel inside. Or in rocket-boxes.

Snow Tires

Fresh snow tires are awesome, turning your everyday vehicle into a Finnish rally car. But snow tires have very soft rubber. But word from my mechanic is that they wear fast when heated -- as when used on dry pavement at freeway speeds above 70.

It seems like I only get 2 or 3 good years of snow grip from snows. Our winters now have more dry pavement than they used to but every week or so we get significant fresh snow, so it's better to be safe. An All-Season tire might be serviceable with AWD, but is so much less fun in proper snow. Hakkapeliittas and Blizzaks are still the ticket.

Minivan Pride

My minivan looks like a tornado hit it for most of each winter. I carry all the skis, gear, and apparel I might need. ...And that's a lot. Plus I haul goodies that those who I run into might want to borrow or buy. On any given day this can amount to a mound of a dozen pairs of skis laying up the center of the van.

Being set up to spend the night in a parking lot before an outing is pretty clever. Quite a few ski bums have bunk-platforms built up above the floor. Ski gear under, on the floor. Foam pad on the bunk: ready, set, go!

Home Style

Keeping gear orderly at home is a fun challenge. Boots out of the way. But everything also needs to dry. Skis and poles always want to fall over. Find a good place to set up storage and drying racks for everything! ...It's time for winter gear pride! You might consider a storage set-up that you and visitors can see and admire in addition to keeping it all out of the way. I like setting up a rack in the yard by the front door.

A minivan can get that lived-in look during an awesome ski season. Great for hauling everything you and your friends might need.

Ski Bags

Winter life on the move, to and fro skiing, can mean piles of jumbled gear if you're not careful. A ski bag is helpful. Ideally, it has separate areas for skis and poles. A duffle for your other gear, a separate bag, maybe mesh, or a separate part of your duffle, is handy for damp gear after an outing.

Then there's the Car Bag for goodies, snacks and cables up front while you drive. Tame the beast! It takes care to avoid having to deal with a Tornado Monster afterward.

I've had the same two large hockey bags for decades (since college) for road-trips of any size.

Then we have packs and fannypacks for fun while we're actually out and about...

Vintage style....

What's Up with Waxing?

Once you catch the ski thrill, you'll want to use ski wax and bring it with you on outings. A little can add a lot of fun. Sure, most times you might blow it off, but you'll at least want to have some around.

There is all sorts of technical how-to online about waxing, from simple to complicated. And anyone who knows how to ski can fill you in. It's not hard, but I'm not going to get into the step-by-step of it here. I'm sticking to the big picture.

Apply some paste-type glide wax for the tips and tails and for the grip section of nowax skis, if you want to keep it simple. Or you can step it up and iron in some glidewax (then scrape it off and brush it). You'll want various kickwaxes if you're striding on waxable skis.

Why do you want wax? Well, skis glide faster and/or kick better when they're waxed. Glidewax gives glide, and gripwax also gives glide. It's a tag-team.

When skis are well waxed they're like magic! You kick and have perfect grip up any hill. You then fly along on each glide like you're on angel's wings. Total traction yet also zero friction: how can this be? … It's the miracle of wax!

And this applies to all temperatures and kinds of snow! It's truly amazing. There's a way to make skis fly and grip no matter what's on the ground.

But you can keep it simple or you can run it as far as you like into the world's deepest rabbit hole. Personally, I like to grab whatever low-hanging fruit I can and usually spend a few minutes to get the main part of the easiest chunk of free fun from my skis.

The Concept

The basic concept is that snow is a crystal. When it's warm, it's soft and needs a soft wax for it to grip into when the ski stops then lets go when the ski moves. When it's cold the crystals are hard and will clog up a soft wax but will bite into a hard wax and then shear off when the ski glides.

There are many awesome nuances to this. Like, new snow crystals have sharper points even when warm. Old snow that's cold is tough but rounded.

Basically, if your skis are sticking, use a harder wax. If they're slippy, use a softer wax.

The glidezones never want grip, but glide has its many nuances, too.

Any kickwax that is too hard for the snow crystals will glide: that's why in the days of wood skis before glidewax was invented people just used a harder kickwax

on their tips and tails. Or since all kickwax can both grip and glide they would just use the right wax on the whole length of the ski: when they pressed, it gripped; when they moved it would glide. What a wonderful two-faced substance!

But there's more: when a ski glides over snow it makes friction and heats the snow and creates a thin layer of water. The friction is less when the base repels the water electrostatically. The more repellence the more the water beads up into rounder beads, pushing the ski off the snow. The colder it is the harder the wax has to be to repel the water. Chemical properties also affect repellence.

That's not all! There's also static and dirt! The drier the snow the more static electricity can be generated by the friction of gliding: a better wax also creates more electrical repellence. And all snow has impurities. Old snow is often downright dirty. This can build up in the wax and hurt the kick and glide. Some wax resists dirt more.

Skis also grip and glide because of how their plastic bases are prepped other than by waxing. The gripzone is sanded so it grabs wax better. And it is desirable that glidezone has some *structure*. Tools are used to put fine grooves in the glidezone called rills. This all helps reduce water suction and static.

The Magic

Those who've been caught by the ski-bug and wax-bug for long enough mutate linguistically: when it's a sunny winter day, moderate temps, fresh snow, they smile and think: "Ooh, what an awesome Blue day!" --And they don't mean the color

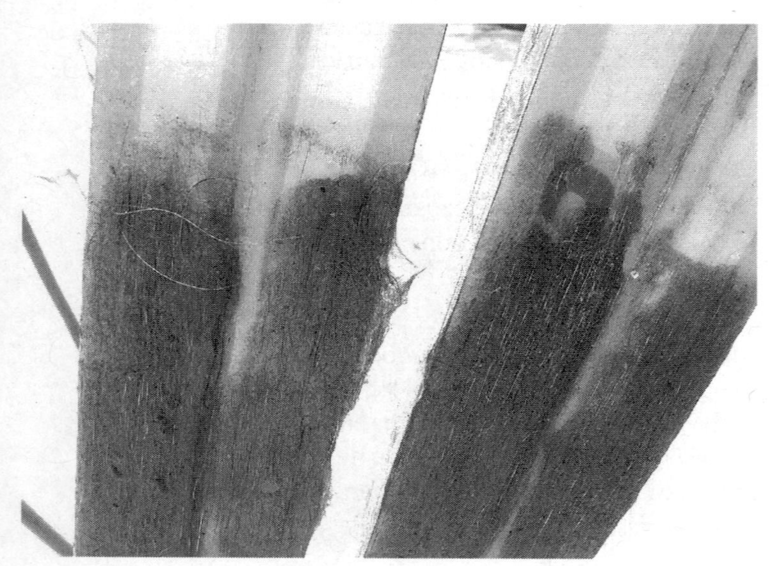

of the sky. If it's colder they might think "Interesting. Kinda squeaky, but it seems sweet. I'm thinking straight-on Green." Yeah, the freaks start thinking of life in terms of wax. You know how the eskimos have 30 words for snow? Yeah, skiers, too...

Here's a big point: Most of us live in modest terrain. And most of us have been subjected to low snow in recent decades. So, the interesting concern for lovers of winter fun is: How do you get the most from the least? ...Easy! Wax those skis! Turns mellow into exciting.

For skating you only use glidewax – good wax makes you feel like you're on ice skates only you're swooping over hill and dale with a breeze on your face from how fast you're going.

In both classic and skating when skis are fit right and waxed right they can seem to disappear from under you, replaced by free flowing glide ...Nice!

That said, many folks just skip it. They leave the same wax on their skis from year to year. The next season rolls around, they hit the snow, they have fun, why bother. Who has the time? Blue wax kicker on waxer skis tends to work for most of a winter.

You can keep waxing simple or you can go whole hog. It's all good!

However, the more that our winters become fickle and weather romps up and down around freezing, the more the nowax skis shine. But even no-waxers go better with care, like glide-waxing tips and tails, and treating the grip portion.

Then with trail skiing on technical singletrack with a lot of tricky up's and down's as long as your skis grip going up you might actually not care how well they glide on the way down. Your glidewax concern tapers off.

But… If the ski jones ever bites you a bit harder than that... If you're getting less snow of a wider variety and don't want to miss any of it… If you want to fly like a bird and enjoy the full miracle of skiing, waxing will take you there. Thankfully, you don't need to fuss much to get most of the perks.

XC skiing seems to get slammed because waxing requires learning. ... Hello? What worthwhile activity is any different? Video games have a myriad of details that users are happy to learn. Why not consider the lore of skiing as one of its virtues.

Like everything, you can take charge of waxing and blow off anything you care to. Everyone learns their own tricks.

For better chances at the race podium it helps to get technical, work precisely and keep records. But if that's not you, who cares! It can be disappointing when races seem like waxing competitions, but if you want to play in the deep end of the pool it comes with the territory. Thankfully quite often it's straightforward. Though it can take at least an hour to prep skis for a race. Many racers find this part to be meditative. …Getting ready for the race. They also often do it with friends, everyone getting psyched, have a beer, put on the tunes.

To have a nice day-trip outing it's usually worth it to prep your skis. This is also the time to ensure your skis aren't damaged.

If you want to race without waxing worry you'll need to join our Trail Skiing

Revolution. Trail skiing is about skill.

But groomed racing is another story. Discovering a rocket-fast wax right before a race is like getting a superpower. Thankfully, each major wax brand posts public info about what to do for waxing each weekend in each region. And there's all sorts of help online. Today there's no excuse for not knowing what to do, except getting lost in the forest of advice.

What is ski wax, anyway? It's a frickin' mystery. It's a proprietary secret for every wax maker. When someone starts a new line of waxes the first thing they do is shut their mouth. Nobody knows how they do any of it! Sure, we know the basic chemical, hydrocarbon, but that's like saying wine is water, sugar and alcohol. It would be awesome if there was a good home-brew option for making ski wax.

What's more after you apply glidewax, you scrape it off! Then brush it out so it's really gone. What the heck? It's like you're doing a big labor-intensive, expensive bunch of nothing to your skis!

And with kickwax, if you put it on thin and buff it good, or iron it in, it, too, can become invisible! Yet if done right it'll be both grip the snow perfectly for zooming up the hills and glide perfectly for zooming down. So after your skis are ready you might look at them and it looks like there's nothing on them! …Mystery!

Here's something freaky… It so happens that the toxic chemical fluorine really repels water when it is applied to a ski. Other chemicals might repel water as well but they are harder to apply to a ski mixed with compounds of varying hardnesses like wax which are meant to mesh with differing temperatures. Even fluorine barely wants to stick to a ski base. It has to be heated very hot to adhere well. Smoking hot, in fact. Sadly, the vapors can slowly kill you, so people who wax fast skis wear respirators. And, really, should work outside. Fluorocarbon wax also is expensive. A few grams of pure fluoro powder can cost over $100 and is good for a few pairs. So, many people are happy to use only cheap and safe hydrocarbon wax for their skis. It glides good and repels water nicely.

Wax gurus know that air temperature and snow temp are different things. But hobbyists can gauge humidity fairly well just by seeing if a snowball is easy to make and how juicy it seems.

Waxing is a game that rewards those who pay attention. In the world of racing it also rewards those who spend a lot of time and money, including hiring waxing technicians and buying many pairs of skis.

It's fun learning about wax. Well, for some people, anyway. Many enthusiasts go at it like laboratory technicians, though I'm not sure how much potential that has for popularizing winter fun. It can be a more casual, though. It's neat learning the kinds of wax you like. Some waxes have pine-tar in them and smell good. At least a couple different famous wax technicians freely share their inside information online, such as Zach Caldwell at Caldwellsport.com and the folks at Boulder Nordic Sport. The Eagle River Nordic shop also releases data on skis and waxes.

Thanks for reading! I hope you enjoy your winter! … JP